Sāḍholāl Lectures on Nyāya

Sri Garib Das Oriental Series No. 178

Sādholāl Lectures on Nyāya

by

Ganganath Jha

Sri Satguru Publications
A Division of
Indian Books Centre
Shakti Nagar, Delhi
INDIA

Published by :
Sri Satguru Publications
Indological and Oriental Publishers
A Division of
Indian Books Centre
40/5, Shakti Nagar,
Delhi-110007
(INDIA)

First Edition : Allahabad 1912 - 1916
Second Edition : Delhi 1994

ISBN 81-7030-402-4

PRINTED IN INDIA

Contents

CHAPTER 1

Introductory

From the standpoint of the ancient Indian philosopher, what every intelligent being in this world seeks is the means of knowing that which would accomplish what he desires. What man desires may be roughly grouped under two heads–the visible and the invisible. So far as the visible is concerned, he knows from the experience of older men, that his visible purposes are served by such visible means as eating, drinking and the like; and for the knowledge of these, therefore, he does not stand in need of any Scripture or Philosophy; we do not need Philosophy to tell us that when there is dirt on our body we should take a bath, or that when we are hungry we should eat. But in regard to the unseen or invisible purposes–such for instance, as the attaining of heaven and Final Release from the process of birth and rebirth–the perceptive power of man is obscured by that ignorance which is the chief factor of human limitations; and this obscuration of ignorance can be dispelled only by the light of Philosophy. Thus it is that it is incumbent on every intelligent person to make a thorough study of Philosophy; not indeed for purposes of mere speculation, but for the purpose of finding out the means for accomplishing his real *summum bonum*; this also not solely for his own benefit, but also for the helping of other fellow-beings who may be bent upon a similar quest; so that the vocation of the philosopher need not be entirely selfish, as has often been remarked.

Philosophy has been defined as *'viḍyāsṭhāna,' i.e.,* the *sṭhāna,* 'substratum, source, fountain-head,' of *'viḍyā,'* Science or Knowledge. For the Hindu, unmindful as he is of the ordinary objects of the world, with which he is concerned for a very short time,—so short indeed that one life on earth may be only the millionth part of a second in the hour of the man's life on Earth,—any science that helps only in the acquirement of knowledge of the physical objects, is not worth the name. For him that alone is real *Science* or *Viḍyā* which helps him to find what will accomplish his purposes relating to ultra-mundane existence; that is, in simple language, that which will make known to him the methods whereby he may attain to a life of entire freedom from pain of all sorts. The physical Sciences also are 'science' only in so far as they discover and make known the means of escaping from pain in this world; but what is Science for the Hindu is only that which discovers the means of avoiding pain absolutely, without fear of recurrence. This method can, according to the Hindu, be found only in the Veda; so that that branch of knowledge alone can be regarded as 'Science' which helps one to find out and grasp and put into practice what is laid down in the Veda.

In view of this the great law-giver Yājñavalkya (1.3) lays down fourteen Sciences: (1) the Ṛigvēḍa; (2) the Yajurvēḍa; (3) the Sāmavēḍa; (4) the Aṭharvavēḍa; these four directly laying down the means of accomplishing such ends of man as heaven and deliverance; (5) the Ḍharmashāsṭra Smṛiṭis; these are supplementary to the Vedas, explaining in greater detail what is already contained in the Vedas; and thus these also serve to indicate the means of accomplishing the said purposes of man; (6) Iṭihāsa and Purāṇa help our understanding of the Veda, and also, by means of high-flown descriptions, render attractive the means laid down in the Veda; (7) Grammar; (8) Astronomy; (9) Phonetics; (10) Prosody; (11) Lexicon–Philology, (12) Ritual; the last six serve to help us to understand the real meaning of the words and phrases contained in the Vedas; and thereby contribute, though indirectly, to our knowledge of the means of accomplishing our purposes; (13) Science of Interpretation, Exegetics; the Vedas being extensive, and more than one passage bearing upon single subjects, it becomes necessary to ponder over these several passages, and deduce from them a cogent idea of what really is meant by the Veda; and thus the Mīmāmsā, which embodies the methodology of interpretation, comes useful; and indirectly helps us to understand what the Veda really says as to the means of attaining what we desire; (14) Science of Reasoning, Nyāya; without the help of reasoning we cannot, in the first place, prove the authoritative character of the Vedas; and until this character is proved, one cannot have any confidence in what is laid down in these; and without sufficient confidence no intelligent person could ever bring himself to undertake the highly elaborate, expensive and inconvenient processes prescribed in the Vedas; hence the Science of Reasoning becomes a most essential factor in the Philosophy of Knowledge conducive to the accomplishment of man's highest purposes. And inasmuch as the very authority of the Veda rests entirely upon this Science, it has been called the 'Illumination of all Sciences', प्रदीप: सर्वविद्यानाम् (Vāṭ. Bhā., p. 7.)

Though all the Hindu philosophical systems, 'heterodox' as well as 'orthodox,' are entitled to be classed as 'Science of Reasoning,' yet on account of the perfect account that the Logicians provide of the usefulness of the subject, we are led to exclude all those philosophies which do not accept and lay stress upon the authority of the Vedas; as it has been pointed out that the real use of the Science of Reasoning lies in its affording proof of the trustworthy character of the Veda. This serves to exclude all the 'Non-Vedic' philosophies and focusses our attention on the Nyāya-Shāsṭra, which thus comes to be regarded as the 'Science of Reasoning' *par excellence*—all the other Vedic Philosophies depending upon the Nyāya, so far as the details of the reasoning-process are concerned.

Another name given to this Science is *'Ānvīkṣikī,'* which denotes that which deals with the *'anu-īkṣaṇa,'* 'subsequent examination,' of what has been learnt by Perception and from the Scriptures; *i.e.,* Inference; and the philosophy propounded by Gauṭama alone is entitled to this name, as the details of Inference are not found worked out in detail in any other philosophy. And to this extent the popular conception of *Nyāya* as 'Logic' does not appear to be very wide of the mark.

The Nyāyamañjarī (pp. 4-5) raises an interesting question on this point. It has been urged that without the help of the Science of Reasoning the authority of the Veda cannot be established; and again that the philosophy of Gauṭama alone represents the real 'Science of Reasoning;' now the question arises—In what manner was the authority of the Veda proved prior to Gauṭama? Certainly the Veda is very much older than the Sūṭra of Gauṭama. The answer given is that the Science of Reasoning itself, along with all the rest of the Sciences, is as old as the Vedas, coeval with these; we have come to associate it with the name of Gauṭama, not indeed because Gauṭama was the first to discover the Science, and there was no Reasoning before him; but because his work provides the most satisfactory account of the subject. Just as Jaimini is called the 'founder of Mīmāmsā,' not because there was no Mīmāmsā before him, or Pāṇini is called the 'founder of Grammar', not because there was no Grammar before him; but simply because these writers have given the most clear and concise account of their respective *shāsṭras.*

Many attempts have been made to fix the historical relationship among the several Indian Philosophies. But to my mind, there is no strict historical sequence among them. All appear to have grown side by side. Through every one of them there runs the same religious incentive. Every one of them has for its aim, final emancipation; every one accepts 'true knowledge' as the means of that emancipation. Where the difference lies is only in the points of specialisation. The Pūrva-Mīmāmsā makes it its special business to evolve principles of exegetics; the Uṭṭara-Mīmāmsā or Vēḍanṭa leaves the things of the ordinary world, and concentrates its attention on ultimate realities only; the Sāṅkhya devotes itself to the study of material evolution, tracing the development of things out of Primordial Matter; the Yoga studies the methods whereby one could realise in actual experience the ultimate reality dealt with by the Vēḍānṭa; the Nyāya specialises itself over the discovering of those principles that should govern all right-thinking and reasoning; and the Vaishēṣika deals only with the things as they are found in our every-day life. It is true that later writers on the several systems have imported other matters also into the field of study; but in the main each system has its own special field; and as such each will always stand in need of the other. So long as all systems declare 'Emancipation of the Soul' as the *summum bonum*; they need the thorough-going distinction between Soul and Matter drawn by the Sāṅkhya; the Vēḍānṭa, so long as it has to depend on Vedic texts, cannot do without the principles of interpretation evolved by the Pūrva-Mīmāmsā; none can ignore the principles of right reasoning dealt with by Nyāya; and so on. There is thus a close inter-relation among the various systems of philosophy that have grown in India; and each has to be supplemented by the other. Of course there must have been some sort of a sequence among the works, the Sūṭras and the commentaries; but the philosophies themselves, the ideas underlying each system, must have grown side by side. They are all coeval with the mind of man; and it does not appear very unreasonable or absurd when the Indian claims eternality for his philosophies.

The above may sound somewhat chimerical to the student of Indian Philosophies who is conversant with the later philosophical literature, wherein they have met with acrimonious disputations, not unmixed with the far from agreeable epithets like *dēvānām priyaḥ, mūdḥay* and so forth, addressed by the upholder of one doctrine to that of another; and the number of works—the *Shaṭaḍūṣaṇī,* the *Chaṇḍamāruṭa* and the *Khaṇḍanas*—dealing entirely with the demolishing of each other. But the fact of the matter is that all later writers have laid stress upon non-essentials, and have strayed far away from the essentials—a procedure which, adopted in whichsoever field of thought and action, always leads to misunderstanding and friction. In order to show that the several philosophies do not differ in essentials, we shall have to go into minute details, for which the present does not appear to be a suitable occasion. I am going to take up only a few of the more important matters. (1) The Sāṅkhya and the Pūrva-Mīmāmsā have been described as 'Atheistic' and as such irreconcilable with the Theistic? systems of the Yogā, the Nyāya and the Vedānta. Now, are the Sāṅkhya and the Pūrva-Mīmāmsā truly atheistic? I am inclined to think they are not; because they do not make mention of a personal God, it does not necessarily follow that they deny Him. The Sāṅkhya made it its special business to draw the much-needed line of demarcation between Matter and Spirit, Prakṛiṭi and Puruṣa, and to describe the evolution of the entire world of mind and matter from the one principle of Primordial Matter; and it posited also a number of sentient beings, in accordance with the form in which sentience is found manifested in the world; beyond that it did not go; it did not make it its business to determine the inter-relation between the multitudinous manifestations of the sentient faculty. With regard to a personal creator, all that the Sūṭra says is that the existence of such a being cannot be *proved;* a position from which it will be extremely difficult to differ. So much for the Sāṅkhya. As regards the Pūrva-Mīmāmsā, we do not find a personal creator mentioned anywhere in the Sūṭras: in fact the Sūṭra does not enter into the question of the constitution of the universe at all. Its avowed business was to find out what the duty of man in this world is, and from whence it could be learnt and its conclusion on this point is that man's duty consists of all those acts that the Veda lays down as bringing about some desirable result; and the *Soul* also is simply put forward as the permanent being possessing the body, to whom the results of actions accrue; it is true that it posits a number of deities. but this it does only by way of providing for personalities to whom the prescribed offerings were to be made: an offering would not be an offering unless it were made to some one; and it is only as recipients of sacrificial offerings that the deities appear in Mīmāmsā literature. It does not go beyond these Gods, to any single Supreme deity or God, as the postulating of such a God would not in any way help in the grasping of the precise nature of those duties for enquiring into which the Shāsṭra was propounded. Then finally we have to examine the inter-relation of the Vēḍānṭa and the Nyāya. Here also we find that on almost all points—except upon the exact position of the atom in the constitution of *matter*—the Vēḍānṭa agrees with all the doctrines of Nyāya; the difference comes when the Vēḍānṭa declares the entire phenomenal world to be unreal. Astounding as this difference appears to be on the surface, it ceases to be so when we come to understand what this 'unreality' means. The Vēḍanṭin admits the *vyāvahārikī saṭṭā,* the practical or empirical reality, of all things: and it is only the ultimate metaphysical reality that it denies to them. Now the

Naiyāyika, who is the most thorough-going exponent of Realism, will find that if the practical reality of things is conceded to him, that is all that he stands for; if for all practical purposes the things are real, what more does the Naiyāyika want? It is enough for his explanation of all our conceptions and experiences. Then as regards the Creator, the Vēḍāntin also admits him; the difference comes only when he stretches his unifying intuition further and finds a Being, purely metaphysical, beyond Ishvara, the Creator of the world. The Nyāya nowhere denies the possibility of such a being; its business was to find a correct explanation of the facts of the world as they present themselves to us; and for this purpose it need not have gone beyond the Creator. Thus then, we find that while some philosophies confine themselves to 'nature,' others soar from 'nature unto nature's God;' and there is one which soars still higher, till it reaches the highest that it is within the power of man's intuition to reach; and there is no inherent antagonism among them. Of course when once we begin to lay stress upon the endless details–mostly non-essential–we find many differences; but the philosophical mind should always rise above minor non-essentials, and fix upon the essentials.

For the modern student, the study of *Nyāya* is more interesting and useful than that of the other systems; as the principles of right reasoning are as necessary in the daily life an thought of the man of the 20th century as they were to that of the pre-Christian days.

The earliest propounder of the Nyāya system of philosophy as known to us is Gauṭama, also known as 'Akṣapāḍa.' All that we know of the personality of the writer is from Vālmiki's Rāmāyaṇa; from this ancient epic we learn that Gauṭama lived in a hermitage in Miṭhilā; this hermitage or 'āshrama' is still known as 'Gauṭama-kunḍa' or 'Ahalyā-sṭhāna;' a place situated in the modern district of Darbhanga, about 20 miles to the N.W. of the town of that name. All that one sees in that place is a small tank known as 'Gauṭama-kuṇda', 'the Tank of Gauṭama,' and a finely built temple of Rāmachanḍra. How Rāmachanḍra came to be connected with the place is described in the Rāmāyaṇa. Gauṭama, in a fit of anger at his wife Ahalyā, cursed her to be turned into stone; and on regaining his calmness he ordained that she would regain her body, when she would be touched by the seventh incarnation of Viṣṇu in the shape of Rāma. When Rāma was being taken by Vishvāmiṭra to Miṭhilā, in view of matrimony, this sage showed to him the hermitage and the stone-image therein placed, and ṭold him the story of Gauṭama and Ahalyā. Advised by the Sage, Ramā touched the image; whereupon Ahalyā regained her body and was translated into heaven.

As to the origin of the name 'Ākṣapāḍa' by which also Gauṭama is known, there are two stories current among Pandits: (1) Gauṭama was so entirely taken up by philosophical contemplation that even during his walks he could not turns his mind away from abstruse philosophical problems; one day while having his mind thus engaged, he fell into a well, which he did not see; it was with difficulty that people got him out of the well; since then, in order to guard against such accidents, God, in his mercy, gave to the sage another pair of eyes in his feet, which would enable him to see things, also when his original eyes would be closed in philosophic contemplation. In view of these 'eyes,' *'akṣa,'* in his 'feet,' *'pāḍa,'* the sage came to be called *'akṣapāḍa,'* 'one who has eyes in his feet.' (2) Another story, related by Mahāmahopāḍhyāya Chanḍrakānṭa Ṭarkālaṅkāra in his preface to the *Nyāyakusumāñjali,* is as follows: Gauṭama had, among his pupils, Vyāsa, who subsequently wrote the Vēḍānṭa or Brahma-Sūṭras; in the second *aḍhyāya* of his work, the pupil referred to the system of his preceptor in terms of disrespect; stigmatising it as one of those philosophies that are 'not accepted by the learned,' *'shiṣṭāparigraha'* (Brahmasūṭra II.1-12). The preceptor was so angry at this that he said he would never look with his eyes on a pupil who had behaved so disrespectfully towards him. On hearing of this Vyāsa went over to him, and prostrating himself at his feet, begged forgiveness, and vowed that he would never move from that position until he had been forgiven and until the preceptor had shown his forgiveness by looking upon him with eyes of affection. The Teacher, moved to pity, and yet unable to revoke his former declaration, caused a new pair of eyes to appear in his feet; and with these eyes he looked upon Vyāsa, who was thereby satisfied.

From this tradition Gauṭama, the writer of the Nyāya Sūṭras would be a senior contemporary of Vyāsa, the author of the Vēḍānṭa-Sūṭras.

As for ascertaining the exact date of Gauṭama, I confess at the very outset that I have not much faith in most of the reasonings that are propounded by writers in this connection; and except when the Author himself mentions the date of his writing–as in the case of Vāchaspaṭi Mishra–or speaks of his work as having been written under orders from a certain king whose date is known–as in the case of Viḍyapaṭi Thakkura–I cannot bring myself to believe in any exact dates being assigned to writers, merely on the strength of reasonings, which presume and presuppose a great deal more than what is strictly warrantable. Yet for those who feel interested in such matters, I append what Pandit Mahadeva R. Bodas of Bombay says on the age of Gauṭama (Journal of the Bombay Branch of the Royal Asiatic Society, No. LIII, Vol. XIX]. *Inter alia* I shall go on adding what my own ideas on each argument adduced are.

Says Pandit Mahadeva R. Bodas–

> "That Gauṭama is posterior to Buddhism is evident on its face; for Buddhistic doctrines are expressly mentioned therein."

If by this it is implied that the work was written after the Sixth Century B.C., that is after the great 'Buḍḍha' Shauḍḍhoḍani, the argument does not justify the conclusion. As it is well-known, from all available sources that there have been many 'Buḍḍhas' before *the* great Buḍḍha; and what are called 'Buddhistic doctrines,' these were in evidence even prior to that great Teacher, who himself declared that it was not his business to propound a new system of philosophy.

Mr. Bodas proceeds—

> "It is also later than the latter part of the Fifth Century B.C., the time of Bādarāyaṇa's Brahmasūṭras, which, while refuting *Vaishēṣika* doctrines, make no mention of the cognate school of *Naiyāyikas.*"

This again is not convincing. In the first place it presupposes an exact date for the Brahmasūtras, which, to my mind, is presuming too much. Secondly the mere fact of Nyāya doctrines not having been specially traversed by the Vēḍānta-Sūṭras does not prove anything positive. The Vaishēṣika had to be refuted, along with the Sāṅkhya, as both of these, holding the original cause of the world to be non-intelligent, *achēṭana,* were found to be opposed to the very basic principle of the Vēḍānṭa: such was not the case with Nyāya, which admits an intelligent God as the cause of the Universe; and so far is in agreement with the Vēḍānṭa; the only difference lying in this that the Nyāya stopped short of the personal creator, and did not go up to the Impersonal Source of all Being. But so long as it did not expressly deny such a Being, the Vēḍānṭa had not much cause to quarrel with it. As for difference in minor details, such details of all systems the Brahmasūtra brushes off by the Sūṭra wherein it rejects all that is शिष्टापरिग्रह, not accepted by the learned. And lastly, according to tradition, the writer of the Brahmasūṭra was a pupil of the writer of the Nyāyasūṭra; hence also he could not directly attack the views of his teacher.

Mr. Bodas proceeds—

"Goldstucker says that both Kāṭyāyana and Paṭañjali knew the Nyāya-sūṭras ('Pāṇini', p.157). Now Paṭañjali is said to have written ḥis great work in 140 B.C., (Ibid. p. 234); but Kāṭyāyana's date is not so certain. According to a story told in the *Kaṭhāsariṭsāgara, Kāṭyāyana* was a pupil of Upavarṣa and a minister of King Nanḍa, who reigned about 350 B.C. Goldstucker makes light of the authority of the Kaṭhāsariṭsāgara; but it is hard to believe that such a story could have got currency without some sort of foundation. If the story is true, the Nyāyasūṭras would have to be placed before 350 B.C. Kāṭyāyana's date is now generally taken to be about the middle of the fourth century B.C.; and so Gauṭama will have to be placed before that time. There is another fact which confirms this conclusion. Shabara Svāmin, the scholiast on Jaimini's Sūṭras, often quotes an ancient author whom he calls 'Bhagavān Upavarṣa,' and who must, therefore, have lived a long time before him. This Upavarṣa is said to have written Commentaries on both the Mīmāmsā-Sūṭras. Our story makes him live in Pātalipuṭra during the reign of King Nanḍa, *i.e.*, about 350 B.C. (See Puruṣaparīkṣā of Viḍyāpaṭi Thakkura). If he be the same as the reputed teacher of Kāṭyāyana above mentioned, he must have lived in the first part of the fourth century B.C. Now a passage quoted by Shabara Svāmin from the Commentary of this Upavarṣa shows that he was intimately acquainted with Gauṭāma's system and largely adopted its doctrines. Gauṭama's work therefore must have been composed before the third century B.C.; that is, it belongs to the 4th century B.C."

This last argument again assumes too much; it assumes, for instance, that the doctrines of the Nyāya had no existence before Gauṭama wrote his Sūṭras; and Mr. Bodas has himself controverted this view (on p. 325 of the Journal) where he remarks rightly—"Gautama was certainly not the pioneer. The very fact that he has evolved a logical system, complete and well-knit in all essential respects, would lead us to suspect that he must have used materials left by his predecessors and profited by their errors." Now one may ask—what is there to preclude the conjecture that the above-mentioned Upavarṣa also was cognisant with these old 'materials' and was not indebted to Gauṭama for them?

I have quoted the above at length and annotated it only with a view to provide an instance of how these matters are generally dealt with and what degree of reliance one should be justified in placing on them.

Like all other Sūṭras, the Sūṭras of Gauṭama had many commentators; but the oldest one that has come down to us is the commentary, or Bhāṣya, by Vātṣyāyana, who refers, in his work, to 'other explanations,' which shows that there were earlier commentaries, and more than one. As regards the name of this commentator, people have held different opinions. It has been held that 'Vāṭsyāyana' is only a patronymic, meaning, 'of the family of Vatṣa;' the real name of the writer was 'Pakṣilasvāmin,' as mentioned by Vāchaspaṭi Mishra in his commentary on the *Vārṭika;* so that the writer of the Bhāṣya known as the *'Vāṭsyāyanabhāṣya,'* is 'Pakṣilasvāmin, a descendant of Vaṭsa.' Others have held that 'Vāṭṣyāyana' is his personal name, and 'Pakṣilasvāmin' is the name of the writer of the *Vārṭika.* But this latter view is opposed to the express declaration of Vāchaspaṭi Mishra; who in the beginning, speaks of the writer of the Bhāsya, as 'Pakṣilasvāmin,' and at the end of his work as 'Vaṭsyāyana;' from which it is clear that the writer of the Bhāṣya is Pakṣilasvāmin, the *Vāṭsyāyana.*

For regarding 'Pakṣilasvāmin' as only another name for Vāṭsyāyana we have the authority of a lexicographical work, the *Abhiḍhānachinṭāmaṇi,* which reads—

वात्स्यायने मल्लनागः कुटिलश्चणकात्मजः

द्रामिलः पक्षिलस्वामी विष्णुगुप्तोऽङ्गुलश्च सः ।

By this verse our Bhāṣyakāra becomes identified with *Chāṇakya,* the well-known minister of Chanḍragupṭa, the great King of Magaḍha; and the author of the *Arṭhashāsṭra,* known as *Kautilya-Sūṭra,* a work on the science of political administration, just brought to light in Mysore, and published in the Mysore Oriental Series. Thus, if reliance can be placed upon the said lexicon, the time of *Bhāṣya* becomes fixed with a certainty rare in the annals of Indian literary history.

Just as Pakṣilasvāmin, 'of the family of Vaṭsa,' is the writer of the *Bhāṣya,* so also the writer of the *Vārṭika,* the commentary on the *Bhāṣya,* is Uḍyoṭakara, 'of the family of Bharaḍvāja;' and 'Bhāraḍvāja' is not the name of the writer of the *Vārṭika.* This also is made clear by the fact that Vāchaspaṭi Mishra, in his introductory verses, speaks of the author of the *Vārṭika* as 'Uḍyotakara,' and in his concluding verses, as 'Bhāraḍvāja; which later name has been rightly regarded as a patronymic, meaning of the family of Bharaḍvāja.'

Chanḍrakānṭa Ṭarkālaṅkāra has held that Uḍyoṭakara flourished about a century before or after the beginning of the Christian era. But he does not adduce any proofs in support of this view. It is beyond doubt however that the *Vārṭika* was written very long before 841 A.D., when Vāchaspaṭi Mishra, the commentator on the Vārṭika wrote his *Nyāyasūchīnibanḍha,* wherein he speaks of having written this work in *Samvaṭ* 898, which would correspond to 841 A.D. Vāchaspaṭi Mishra, in his introductory verses, speaks of the 'words of Uḍyoṭakara,' as 'very old.'

Uḍyoṭakara was preceded by the Buddhist logician Diṅnāga, who lived in the 5th Century A.D. And as it was the avowed aim of Uḍyoṭakara (see opening verses of the *Vārṭika*) to guard the philosophy of Gauṭama against the misrepresentations of 'unfair logicians,' identified by Vāchaspaṭi Mishra with Diṅnāga and his followers, it will be safe to assign the Vārṭika to the sixth century A.D.; that it was written long before 635-650 A.D., is proved by the fact of its forming an object of attack by *Ḍharmakīrṭi*, a Buddhist logician who wrote between 635 and 650 A.D., and who defended Diṅnāga against the strictures of Uḍyoṭakara. The date of the *Vārṭika* must be fixed at between 500-600 A.D. This also agrees with the traditional belief that the writer was a contemporary of 'Vikramāḍiṭya,' who is now believed to have flourished in the 6th Century A.D.

We do not know of any other work written by the author of the *Vārṭika;* but Pandit Vinḍhyēshvarī Prasāḍa Dvivēḍin of the Benares Sanskrit College possesses the manuscript of a work known as the 'Varṭika' on the Vaishēṣikasūṭra of Kaṇāda,' called 'Bhāraḍvājavārṭika.' It seems likely that the author of this Vārṭika also is our Uḍyoṭakara, who also is 'Bhāraḍvajā,' of the family of Bharaḍvājā.

Uḍyoṭakarā's *Vārṭika* has been commented upon by Vāchaspaṭi Mishra. We have seen that by his own declaration he flourished in the middle of the ninth century; under the patronage of a king named Nṛiga. We do not know over what part of the country this king ruled. But tradition has it that Vāchaspaṭi Mishra was a Maiṭhila-Brāhmaṇa; who lived somewhere near the Nepal frontier; where we find a village by the name of 'Bhāmā,' which is believed to be named after Bhāmaṭī, the name of Vāchaspaṭi Mishra's daughter, in whose memory he named his commentary on Shaṅkarāchārya's Bhāṣya on the *Brahmasūṭras.* This writer was a man of versatile genius; equally at home in all systems of philosophy. He has left works dealing with every one of the six systems and each one of his works is regarded as an authoritative account of that system. It is believed that he wrote equally lucid accounts of the six 'Atheistic,' systems also; of one of them the name also is mentioned–a commentary on the *'Ohiṭṭavinsaça'* of the well-known Bauḍḍha writer Ḍharamkīrṭi; we have not yet come across a manuscript of this work. But his tradition appears to be unfounded: Vāchaspati Mishra has himself enumerated all his works in the concluding verses of the Bhāmti; here he mentions only the following : (1) *Nyāyakaṇikā,* a work on Pūrva–Mīmāmsā, commentary by Maṇdana Mishra's *Viḍhivivēka* [both published in the Pandit, (2) *Ṭaṭṭvasamīkṣā,* a Vēḍānta work, not yet discovered, (3) *Ṭaṭṭvabinḍu,* a small work dealing with the science of predication, [published in the *Pandit,* (4) Commentary of the *Nyāya-Sūṭras,* evidently, the *Nyāyāvārṭikaṭaṭparya-tika* [published in the Vizianagram Sanskrit Series], [5] commentary on the Sāṅkhya-Shāsṭra, the *Sāṅkyaṭaṭṭvakaumanḍi* [published in many places], (6) Commentary on the *Yogasūṭras,* the *Ṭaṭṭvaishāraḍī,* better known as *'Vachaspaṭya,'* published more than once; and (7) Commentary on the *Vēḍānṭa-Suṭras,* the well-known *Bhāmaṭi* [published in the Bibliothica Indica].

Vāchaspati Mishra's work has been expounded by *Uḍayana,* better known as *Uḍayanāchārya*; and referred to by modern writers as the 'Āchārya.' Uḍayana flourished about the tenth century of the Christian era, and his commentary is known as the *Ṭaṭparyaparishuḍḍhi;'* this is being printed. He is however better known as the author of the *Kusumāñjali* and the *Āṭmaṭaṭṭvavivēka* (better known as '*Bauḍḍhaḍhikkāra*') which two works have been regarded as embodying unanswerable arguments against all forms of Atheism–the Materialistic Atheism of the Chārvāka, the Vedic Atheism of the Mīmāmsaka, the philosophic Atheism of the Bauḍḍha and the Jaina, and the rationalistic Atheism of the Sāṅkhya.

Uḍayāna's works are supposed to contain unanswerable arguments against Atheism; and he is believed to have put the quietus to the atheistic philosophy of the Bauḍḍha, rampant from about 500 A.D. to 1000 A.D.; the attack on Atheism that began with Shaṅkarāchārya is believed to have been carried to its successful issue by Uḍayana; who is, on that account, regarded as the apostle of Theism; and many a story is current among Pandits on this point. It is told, for instance, that on one occasion he went to Puri; and in order to try this devotion, the God would not show himself to him; thereupon the great philosopher is reported to have indignantly addressed the God thus.–

ऐश्वर्यमदमत्तोऽसि मामवज्ञाय वर्तसे। पराक्रान्तेषु बौद्धेषु मदधीना तव स्थितिः॥

'Intoxicated with greatness Thou treatest me with ignominy: but (Thou forgetest that) when the Bauḍḍhas were in power Thy very existence depended upon me.'

After Uḍayana, came Varḍhamāna Upāḍhyāya, who wrote his *Nyāyanibanḍhaprakāsha,* a commentary on Uḍayanācharya's *'Parishuḍḍhi;'* and also commented upon the other works of Uḍayana. With *Varḍhamāna,* the series of works dealing with what is known as 'Prāchīna' or 'older' Nyāya comes to a close.

We have hitherto confined our attention to the Hindu writers on the *Nyāya-Sūṭras.* But we learn from the researches of Mahāmahopāḍhyāya Satish Chandra Viḍyabhūṣāna of Calcutta that Gauṭama's Sūṭras had its followers also among the Bauḍḍhas and the Jainas. But none of these writers appear to have written any commentaries; they wrote logical manuals of their own. The most thorough-going writer among Buddhist logicians was Diṅnāga; whose views formed the main points of attack for later Brāhmaṇa logicians. He wrote the *Pramāṇasamuchchaya.* The chief points of difference however between these logicians were mainly metaphysical; on purely logical points, the differences are not more pronounced than what one finds among the several Brāhmaṇa logicians themselves; at least so far as we can know from the very brief accounts that we have hitherto had of what is contained in the works of the Bauḍḍha logicians.

The *Kusumāñjali* of Uḍayana introduced into the field of Nyāya that spirit of independent thought and reasoning which marks an epoch in the literary history of India. It was Uḍayana who was the pioneer of that Modern School, which, freed itself from the time-honoured grooves of the Sūṭras and betook itself to that rigid course of strict reasoning which, beginning in the *Kusumāñjali* and the *Āṭmaṭaṭṭvavivēka,* reached its final stage in the *Ṭaṭṭrachintāmaṇi* of Gaṅgēsha Upāḍhyāya, a writer who flourished in Miṭhilā, before the fourteenth century. Gaṅgēsha has been regarded as the founder of the *Navya* or modern Nyāya; as henceforth Indian logicians began to drop the study of the Sūṭras, and came to look upon the *Ṭaṭṭvachinṭāmaṇi* as the 'mūla,' or 'text' of their system, which thereupon, attracted the talent of all later writers; the host of commentaries beginning with that of Jayaḍēva or Pakṣaḍhara Mishra in the later part of the 15th century, ending with Gaḍāḍhara. Gaṅgēsha was the founder of the Miṭhilā School of Nyāya, which was succeeded by the Naḍiā School.

The tradition current among the Pandits of Miṭhilā and Naḍia is that before Raghunāṭha Shiromaṇi, who is believed to have flourished, somewhere towards the end of the 16th century, Nyāya was taught only in Miṭhilā; and Maiṭhila Professors were so jealous of the fame of their country that when any foreign students came to learn, they taught them what they had to teach; but when they had finished their study, and were going to return to their country, the teacher made them return to him all the manuscripts from which they had learnt. This went on till the time when a couple of young men came from Bengal, and while undergoing the usual course, took care to commit to memory the principal text-books. One of them fixed in his memory the Kārikās of the *Kusumāñjali;* and another the greater part of the text of the *Ṭāṭṭvachinṭāmaṇi.* On returning to their country, they committed the texts to writing; and thereupon the study of Nyāya began to flourish at Naḍia in Bengal, and the Naḍia School at last supplanted the Miṭhilā School, to such an extent that during the last century, no Maiṭhila logician considered his logical training complete until he had gone over to Naḍia and finished his studies under one of the Bhattāchāryas there.

Though it is the current idea among scholars that Gaṅgēsha is the founder of the modern Nyāya, this does not appear to be strictly accurate. The principal point of difference between the works dealing with 'prāchīna' and 'navya' Nyāya lies in the fact that the former deals with the entire subject-matter of the Sūṭras–treating systematically of all the categories enunciated in the opening Sūṭra; while the moderns have confined their attention to the *pramāṇas* alone, leaving the *pramēyas* either to be dealt with in separate works, or to be explained only as subordinate to the Pramānas. By applying this criterion, we are led to include the logical works of the Jainas and the Bauḍḍhas to the latter school. So that there would be only two schools of Nyāya; though the names प्राचीन and नवीन appear to have been badly chosen. The study of Gauṭama's Sūṭras has never entirely dropped out; and even so late as the 17th century, an independent commentary is found to have been written by Vishvanāṭha. And coming down to our own day we know of a lucid commentary on Vāṭṣyāyana having been written by the late lamented Mahāmahopāḍhyāya Kailāsha Chanḍra Shiromaṇi: of the Sanskrit College, Benares. And on the other hand, as early as the fifth century, we find the Bauḍḍha writer, Diṅnāga devoting his entire work exclusively to the consideration of the Pramāṇas.

There is however one criterion which serves to demarcate very clearly the 'prāchīna' from the 'navya' Nyāya. The earlier works deal with things, while the later ones with only the verbal description or definition of things. The latter do not trouble themselves about the nature of things; they are satisfied if they can evolve a correct definition–लक्षणप्रमाणाभ्यां वस्तुसिद्धिः is their dictum; and to लक्षण and प्रमाण alone they turn. And in their verbal definitions they evince a subtlety and dialectic skill, which to a certain extent, compensates for the paucity of their material; and as providing a means of intellectual training, specially in the domain of correct thinking, and still more correct expression of thought, it is not without its value.

By this criterion then, we shall be justified in dividing Nyāya into three schools–(1) Prāchīna, or *old,* represented by Gauṭama and his commentators; (2) Maḍhyama or Medieval, represented by the Jaina and Bauḍḍha writers, who, though confining their attention to the Pramāṇas, do not give themselves up entirely to the verbal accuracy of their definitions; and (3) Navya or Modern, which deals only with *pramāṇas,* and *lakṣaṇas;* and even here, they give themselves up entirely to the verbal *lakṣana* or definition of things. It has to be borne in mind however that in point of *time,* there are constant overlappings in this division.

CHAPTER II

The Method Adopted by Gauṭama

The method to be adopted by all writers on important subjects has been thus laid down by Vāṭsyāyana (Bhāṣya, p. 9).

'The Shāstra proceeds in three ways—it states the names of things to be dealt with; then it defines those things, indicating the characteristic features of each; and lastly it examines those things, with a view to find out how far each fulfils the conditions of its definition.'

It is this method that has been adopted by Gauṭama in his Sūṭras. In the first Sūṭra we have the mention by name of all the topics that are to be dealt with.

These are—(1) Instrument of Right Cognition, (2) Object of Cognition, (3) Doubt, (4) Motive, (5) Corroborative Instance, (6) Demonstrated Truth, (7) Factors of Syllogistic Reasoning, (8) Hypothetical Reasoning, (9) Definitive Cognition, (10) Discussion, (11) Controversy, (12) Wrangling; (13) Fallacious Reason, (14) Casuistry, (15) Futile Rejoinder, and (16) Clinchers.

Herein we find mentioned every one of the topics that are dealt with by the Sūṭras. And in this connection the question naturally arises—"Why should these sixteen be selected for treatment? There does not appear to be any principle underlying this choice; the list being a most heterogeneous one; it is no wonder that the entire book of Gauṭama is unsystematic and disjointed; and seems to lead to nothing."

It has to be borne in mind that the Nyāya, along with all other systems, is meant to lead to the attaining of the *summum bonum*, the absolute cessation of pain, by means of the true knowledge of the things of the world. And the method adopted by Gauṭama for conveying this knowledge to people is a unique one; it is this uniqueness that confounds people at first sight, when they look upon the list of apparently unconnected things, put forth in the opening Sūṭra. Yet a moment's thought will make it clear that Gauṭama's method is not only unique and novel, but also the most effective.

Gauṭama presupposes the presence of two parties to a discussion and an Umpire; and the method of procedure at a discussion is for the parties to present their views on the point at issue before the Umpire who decides as to the final issue. It is with this view that the sixteen topics have been mentioned by Gauṭama in the way in which we find them in the opening Sūṭra. (1) Whenever there is found a difference of opinion between two persons upon any point, before the discussion can begin, it becomes necessary to ascertain which are the means of cognition or proofs that are admitted by the parties; as unless an understanding is arrived at as to what will be admitted as proof, and what will not be admitted as such, there will be interminable confusion and ground-shifting, and the truth of nothing can be brought home to any party. Thus it becomes necessary to begin with an enumeration of Proofs or Pramāṇas. (2) Next it becomes necessary to ascertain what are the objects the knowledge of the exact nature whereof is necessary for liberation, and over which the difference of opinion and the consequent discussion is focussed; thus it becomes necessary, as the second item in the scheme to mention the 'objects of cognition,' the Pramēyas; and it is 'Pramēya' that comes second in the Sūṭra. (3) When we know what the things are whose knowledge is necessary for salvation, and which, on that account, has to be sought after, we come to ponder over the character of the things; and there arises in our mind a doubt as to their exact nature; without such doubt, no investigation would proceed, doubt being the incentive to all enquiry and investigation. Thus it is '*Samshaya,*' 'Doubt,' that appears *third* in the Sūṭra. (4) Before one takes up a serious and time-consuming investigation he naturally pauses to consider why he should undertake it and what useful purpose would be served by it; hence what comes in as the fourth item in Gauṭama's programme is '*Prayojana,*' 'Purpose,' or 'Motive.' (5) When it comes to the consideration of the Motive, one of the two parties of the discussion comes forward, and while explaining the motive that should urge people to the seeking after knowledge, he states his own view of the case under investigation; and before he actually puts forward his conclusions in a dogmatic manner, he cites a number of instances, without, which his statement would remain incomplete and not easily intelligible. It is on this account that Ḍriṣṭānṭa, 'Instance,' figures as the fifth item on the list. (6) When he is convinced of the effect produced by his citing of the corroborative instances, he puts forward his own conclusions on the point, as 'demonstrated truth;' thus it is the 'Demonstrated Truth' or 'Siḍḍhānṭa' that comes in as the sixth item. (7) In stating his case the first party has made certain assertions; the other party now comes forward and puts to him questions and seeks to obtain from him a clear statement of what his reasons are; and on being acquainted with these, he with a view to criticise these reasonings intelligently, finds it necessary to analyse them, and to find out what premises have been presupposed, what is the probans and what the probandum sought to be proved by it, what the corroborative instance cited; and so forth; as without this thorough analysis it will not be possible for him to detect and expose to the Umpire any fallacies that may be involved in the reasoning of his opponent; hence, the first thing the second party has got to do is to resolve his opponent's reasoning into its several component parts or factors; so '*Avayava,*' 'Factors of Reasoning,' comes seventh on the programme. (8) Finding his reasonings assailed, the first party puts forward further arguments based upon contingencies that would arise if his view; were not accepted; and these, while tending to support his own view, serve also to confute the opposite view; this process has been called 'Ṭarka,' 'Hypothetical Reasoning' which is eighth on the list. (9) The counter-reasonings propounded serve to strengthen the conclusion formerly put forth; and the conclusion thus strengthened comes to be looked upon as the '*Nirṇaya*' or 'definitive cognition' of the thing concerned; and this *Nirṇaya* is the ninth on the list. (10) The Opponent is not satisfied with this; and requests the Umpire to permit a regular discussion on the subject, as without such discussion the real truth cannot be got at; this discussion for the finding out of truth, '*Vāḍa,*' therefore comes next on the list. (11) If the two parties are fair fighters and engage in the discussion with the pure intention of getting at the truth, then after some discussion they will come to an agreement as to the truth, and the matter will end; but it will often happen that they engage in the discussion simply for the purpose of showing off their learning and intelligence and of obtaining victory over one another; in which case, the discussion will go on; each party refusing to accept defeat, and contriving to put forward reasonings and counter-reasonings, not always of the best sort; this improper form of discussion has been called 'controversy,' 'Jalpa,' which is *eleventh* in the Sūtra. (12) For sometime the parties will go on putting forth arguments with a certain amount of fairness and plausibility;

but after a short time, each persisting in his desire for victory over the other, will find the stock of plausible arguments exhausted, whereupon he will begin to make absurd statements, often having no bearing upon the subject under discussion and regardless of the original position taken up; in fact, after some time, the disputants lose all sight of the proposition they have to prove, and concentrate their energies entirely upon the putting forth of arguments or series of arguments and the making of statements simply with a view to confound and silence the other party. This leads to the worst form of Controversy that has been called 'Wrangling,' 'Viṭaṇḍā,' the twelfth on the list. (13) Most of the reasonings that will be propounded in course of this wrangling will be entirely *fallacious,* bristling with what has been called, *Hētvābhāsa* or 'Fallacious Reason,' which thus comes in as the thirteenth name on the list. (14) In addition to these semi-reasonings the disputants will make use of absurd statements and devises to confound the other party: and this will constitute 'Chhala,' 'Casuistry,' the fourteenth name on the list. (15) When a disputant begins to make such loose absurd statements, the audience will begin to feel that he is losing his ground; and that not finding even such arguments as may have the slightest semblance of correct reasoning, he has recourse to what has been called the 'Futile Rejoinder,' '*Jāṭi,*' which is the fifteenth name on the list. (16) Soon after this, all men present are convinced that the proposition put forward by the first party is true and that by the other party false; whereupon the Umpire prevents the second party from further talk; in view of the fact that he has degraded himself by having recourse to artifices that have been called '*nigrahasṭhāna,*' 'position of being stopped,' 'Clincher;' which comes in as the last item of the scheme; this puts a stop to all further discussion. And the people who have been taking part in it, as disputants or Umpires, are convinced as to what is the truth in regard to the things they had undertaken to investigate; and this true knowledge accomplishes the final end of man, emancipation from pain.

We thus see how perfectly systematic and logical Gauṭama is in the method he has adopted.

This is the justification of Gauṭama's enunciation of the 'topics of discussion.' Those who have objected to it, have misunderstood the Sūṭra to embody on enumeration of distinct *paḍārṭhas* or categories. On the very face of it, it is abundantly clear that what we have here is not a classification of categories, but only a list of topics to be dealt with in the Sūṭras. This is clear; as the word 'prameya' itself includes all that can be known, that is, all things; hence if Gauṭama's intention were to provide a list of *paḍārṭhas,*—each distinct by itself, like the Vaishēṣika's enumeration of the six or seven *paḍārṭhas,* where each stands distinct from the rest, he would either not put 'prameya' in the Sūṭra, or having put it, would put in nothing else.

Hence even though all the topics beginning with Doubt will be found to be included under either 'Pramāṇa' or 'Prameya,' yet they have been singled out for special treatment, as they are efficient aids to that Science of Reasoning, Nyāya-Shāsṭra, which accomplishes the *summum bonum* of man. For instance, reasoning cannot proceed over a subject on which there are no doubts; it is only when a certain matter is open to doubt that the help of reasoning is called in to set aside the doubt. Some sort of motive is essential for all human activity; hence the presence of a motive is necessary for reasoning. Examples are great helps to reasoning; the truth of a reasoning is never brought home so strongly by anything else as by a well-known instance. Unless there is some truth regarded by the reasoner as demonstrated, in support of what would we adduce the reasoning? Some demonstrated truth therefore is essential. When the reasoning is put forward to convince another person, it has to be stated in its full form, with all its factors clearly set forth. Hypothetical Reasoning serves the purpose of showing the weakness of views contrary to the truth.

Discussion proper helps to establish the truth by setting aside whatever doubts and misconceptions there may be in the mind of the person to whom the reasoning is addressed. The other two forms of discussion, Controversy and Wrangling, serve to bring conviction to the mind of the simple learner, who may have been confused by the plausible arguments of misguided teachers, whose weakness having been exposed in course of controversy, the learner's mind becomes reassured. A knowledge of the Fallacious Reason is necessary for the purpose of avoiding such reasons in one's own reasoning, and also for that of detecting them in the reasoning of the Opponent. A knowledge of the reamaining three topics, Casuistry, Futile Rejoinder and Clinchers, comes useful in Controversies and Wranglings, in silencing, and exposing the weakness of, persons holding and expounding views contrary to the truth.

Thus the knowledge of every one of the sixteen topics is found to be essential.

CHAPTER III

Pramāṇa and Bhrānti

Pramāṇa

As we have seen above, the first topic that engages Gauṭama's attention is *Pramāṇa;* by which word is meant the *means of cognition,* by which we obtain the cognition, as also the *form of cognition,* whereby we learn the character of the thing cognised. The word is found to be used in both these senses; and the earliest writers have drawn a distinction between these two significations of the word; we shall see this as we proceed.

The word '*pramāṇa*' literally means, the *karaṇa,* the 'principal instrument,' of *pramā,* 'right cognition.' Though there are many things by whose instrumentality cognitions are brought about, yet the word 'pramāṇa' cannot apply to all these; it applies to that only which is the principal instrument, the *sāḍhaka-ṭama,* the best instrument;—that without which it would be impossible to have the cognition. For instance, when we see a tree, what helps us to see it consists of many things—the eyes, the particular shape of the tree, its colour, its position, its size, daylight, and so forth; but it would be possible for us to see the tree, even if it had some other shape, other colours, another size; if it rested in another place, we would see it; but if our eyes were absent, it would be absolutely impossible to *see* the tree; hence it is the eye and its contact with the tree that are recognised as the *karaṇa,* the principal instrument, of the visual cognition of the tree.

The importance of the subject of *Pramāṇa* as bearing on Philosophy is thus stated by Vāṭsyāyana in his Introduction to the *Bhāṣya.*

"The Instruments of Right Cognition must be regarded as rightly effective, because it is only when a thing is known by means of an Instrument of Right Cognition that there is a possibility of its giving rise to fruitful and effective exertion. As a matter of fact, nothing can be known except through an instrument of cognition; nor can fruitful exertion be aroused except when things have been known; as it is only when the agent has cognised a thing by means of an instrument of cognition that he desires either to acquire or get rid of it; and the effort of the agent stimulated by this desire to acquire or get rid of the thing known is what is called 'exertion;' and this exertion is called 'fruitful' when it becomes related to a result; that is to say, when the person putting forth the exertion, on desiring either to acquire or get rid of the thing, comes, by that exertion, actually to acquire or to discard it, his exertion becomes 'fruitful.' The object or thing cognised by means of the instrument of right cognition is of four kinds–*viz.,* either (1) pleasure, or (2) source of pleasure, or (3) pain, or (4) source of pain. These objects of the instrument of cognition are innumerable, owing to the fact of the number of living creatures being infinite. It is only when the instrument of right cognition duly operates with regard to an object that due success can belong–to the 'cogniser,' who then only can have any idea of the object,–to the 'cognised object,' which then only can have its true character known,–and to the 'right cognition,' which then only can lead to the due comprehension of the object; because there is no possibility of the object being accomplished so long as the most effective cause is not present; and it is the Instrument of Cognition that is the most effective cause. 'Cogniser,' *'Pramātṛi'* means that person who is stimulated to exertion by the desire to acquire or discard the object; that by means of which the person obtains the right cognition of the thing is called the 'Instrument of Right Cognition,' *'Pramāṇa':* that thing which is rightly known is called the 'cognised object,' *'Pramēya;'* and the comprehending or knowledge of the thing is called 'right cognition,' *Pramiṭi.'* It is on all these four factors that the real nature of things is dependent for its being accepted or rejected or treated with indifference. Now, what is this 'real nature' of things? It is nothing else but 'being' or 'existence' in the case of that which *is,* and 'non-being' or 'non-existence' in the case of that which *is not.* That is to say, when something that is apprehended as *being* or *existent,* so that it is apprehended as what it really is, and not as something of a contrary nature, then what is thus apprehended constitutes the *true nature* of the thing. And analogously when a non-entity is cognised as such,—*i.e.,* as what it really is, not as something of a contrary nature,—then that which is thus apprehended constitutes the *true nature* of the non-entity. "But how is it possible for the non-entity to be cognised by means of an Instrument of right cognition?" This is possible, we reply; because as a matter of fact, at the time that the *existing* being is cognised, the *non-existing* thing is not cognised. That is to say, there is non-cognition of the non-existing only when there is cognition of the existing; and from this it follows that the non-existing thing is cognised by means of the same Instrument of Cognition by which the existing thing is cognised; the only difference between the existing and the non-existing being that, while the former forms the object of the instrument of cognition directly, the latter does so only indirectly, through something that exists. We illustrate this by reference to a lamp: when the lamp illumines and renders visible something that is visible, that which is not seen in the same manner as that visible thing is regarded as 'non-existing;' the mental process being as follows:—'if the thing existed it would be seen, as it is not seen,—it must be concluded not to exist.' In the same manner, at the time that the existing thing is cognised by an instrument of knowledge, if something else is not equally cognised, we at once regard the latter as non-existing; the mental process being—'if the thing existed it would be cognised,—as it is not cognised, it must be concluded to be non-existent.' Thus we find that the same instrument of cognition which manifests and makes known the existing thing also makes known the non-existing thing."

We shall enter into a little detail as to the conception of Pramāṇa, as accepted by the Naiyāyika.

The questions that arise are—What is Pramāṇa and what is the form or character of Pramāṇa? The name 'Pramāṇa' is given to that entire apparatus, or concatenation of circumstances, which itself partaking of the nature of apprehension, as well as that of what is not apprehension, brings about the correct and certain apprehension or cognition of a thing; that is to say, that whereby is brought about a cognition which pertains to an object, which is free from all doubt and which is not wrong. This shows that Pramāṇa is of the nature of apprehension, as well as of non-apprehension; and its characteristic feature—that which makes the apprehension or non-apprehension capable of being known by the name of 'pramāṇa'—is the character of bringing about such apprehension of things as is *correct, certain* and so forth.

An objection raised against this view is that the word 'Pramāṇa' etymologically means 'the *principal instrument* of right cognition;' and the principalship of an instrument depends upon its being the most important of all the factors that bring about the cognition; and so it is only one of these factors that can be called 'principal'; and any 'entire apparatus,' or 'concatenation of circumstances' can not be called *the principal instrument.*

The answer to this is that it is because in the bringing about of right cognition, the operation of all the factors constituting the apparatus is absolutely necessary,—that we regard the entire apparatus as the *principal instrument;* that which leads to the cognition directly, as well as that which accords but indirect help—the operation of both sets of causes is essential; and that whose operation is essential cannot but be regarded as the *principal instrument;* and as the operation of every one of the factors that form the 'apparatus,' is essential, we regard the entire apparatus as the *principal instrument of cognition.* This is common-sense, pure and simple. The cognition is produced only when all the factors of the apparatus are operative; it is *not* produced when the operation of even one factor out of these is absent; from this it follows that the entire apparatus forms the principal instrument.

It has been held that this Instrument of Right Cognition is of the nature of apprehension and non-apprehension. When we see the horse in the first instance, the cognition is brought about by the instrumentality of the contact of the sense-organ with the mind, and of the Mind with the Soul, as we shall see under Perception; and in this case it is these contacts that constitute the instrument of our perception of the horse and the contact *is not apprehension.* Whereas in the case of inferential cognition, we find that the final cognition is brought about by the cognition of the various factors that enter into the inference, and of the relationship among these; in verbal cognition the cognition is brought about by a previous cognition of words and their meanings; so also analogical cognition is due to the cognition of similarity; and in all these cases certain cognitions enter into the apparatus that leads to the cognition; hence in these cases the Instrument partakes of the nature of cognition or *apprehension.*

In view of the fact that the cognising agent and the cognised object also enter into the apparatus essential for the cognition, the above definition would apply to these also; while as a matter of fact the name 'pramāṇa' should apply to the *instrument,* and not to the agent or the objective. If all were jumbled together under the single conception of '*Pramāṇa,* how could we reconcile this with the four-fold distinction into '*Pramāṭri,*' cogniser, '*pramēya,*' object, '*Pramiṭi,*' cognition, and Pramāṇa or instrument of cognition—made by the Bhāṣya in the introductory notes? For these reasons later logicians have rightly modified the aforesaid definition, which they would read as follows: 'Pramāṇa' is that entire apparatus, *apart from the cognising agent and the cognised object,* which, partaking of the nature of apprehension and non-apprehension, brings about such cognition of the object as is free from uncertainties and mistakes.'

The *Mīmāmsakas* regard the cognition itself as the 'Pramāṇa;' and what it brings about in the object is the character of beings apprehended. This, as we shall see, the Naiyāyika does not accept.

Some philosophers add a further qualification to the cognition that is brought about by the instrumentality of Pramāṇa. In order to call a cognition, 'right,' they lay it down as an essential condition that the cognition be of a thing that is not already known. It is with a view to distinguish 'Right Cognition' from 'Remembrance' that people have added this qualification; but they lose sight of the fact that what makes 'Remembrance' *apramāṇa,* or invalid cognition, is the fact of its being brought about without the actual contact of the object; and not the fact of its object being already known. When I buy a horse, I see it and know it for the first time; the next day when I see it again, the seeing of it, the second visual cognition, of the horse cannot be regarded as *wrong,* simply because the horse is already known to me. Nor is it necessary that each time that I see the horse I perceive something new, not previously known,—which unperceived factor would make the subsequent perception *valid.* Hence if we accept the additional qualification proposed, we would have to reject as invalid all cognitions of all things except the very first one that we may have had.

The Bauḍḍhas would add the qualification that the cognition to be *right* must not be discordant with the thing; that is, it should lead to the thing being got at; *i.e.,* it should serve to show to the cogniser something which would lead him to an activity tending to obtain what is pleasant and desirable, and to discard what is unpleasant and undesirable. As a matter of fact, it is argued, it is only when a certain thing has been shown or made known to the agent by the cognition that he has recourse to that activity which leads him to obtain the thing if it is desirable, or to discard it if it is undesirable; hence the operation of this Pramāṇa upon the thing, consists in its *showing* it; and when it shows it, it makes it got at.

This qualification also is not admissible; as we cognise not only those things that are got at or obtained, but also those that are rejected; how then can we define *Pramāṇa* as that which leads to things *being got at;* and further, no such qualification is possible for the Bauḍḍha; as according to him every object is undergoing destruction every moment; so that what the cognition apprehends cannot be what the cogniser obtains subsequently; hence it is never possible for a cognition to lead to object its being got at.

Lastly, the *Sāṇkhyas* have defined Pramāṇa as the *vṛiṭṭi* or function of the Buḍḍhi, Intellect. They hold that when an object comes into contact with an organ, the organ becomes turned into the shape of that object; and upon the organ thus shaped, the operation of the Buddhi falls; and presents it to the view of the percipient Soul.

This also cannot be accepted. As according to this view that in which the cognition appears, that which obtains the cognition, is the real Buḍḍhi, which is material, inanimate, unconscious; while that to whose view the thing is presented is the conscious Soul; so that the result of the cognition is not in the same substratum as the cognition itself.

The word 'pramāṇa' involves two conceptions–Pramā, or Right Cognition and its Principal Instrument. We must explain these. And as Pramāṇa is only a particular kind of Cognition, we proceed to consider the nature of Cognition in general.

On the present occasion we shall deal with Cognition only as entering into the conception of Pramāṇa; the other details in connection with it we shall explain when we deal with it as one of the Pramēyas. The great division of all knowledge, cognition, state of consciousness, *jñāna, buḍḍhi, praṭyaya,* is, according to the general Indian view (as represented by the Nyāya) into Anubhava and Smṛiṭi. The former term comprises all cognitions (including what we would call states of feeling, experiences of pleasure and pain), which, when presenting themselves to the mind, are strictly *original, i.e.* not reproductions of former cognitions. In this sense, the cognition which we have through sight and touch of a fire burning before us, the idea we have of a fire on a distant hill, owing to an inference based upon the perception of smoke issuing from the hill, and the knowledge of a fire burning somewhere, which we acquire through the statement of a trustworthy person or an authoritative book,–are all of the nature of *anubhava;* such *anubhava* is not necessarily true knowledge or right cognition; it is *anubhava* also when, in dim light, we see a man where there is only a post, or a snake where there is only a rope. *Smṛiṭi* on the other hand, comprises all cases of *representative* cognition, when the cognition before the mind is not at the time originated by one of the 'means of knowledge,'—*Pramāṇa;* but is the mere re-entering into consciousness of a previous cognition.

It will thus be seen that accurately speaking *anubhava* is neither 'direct apprehension,' nor 'direct knowledge,' nor immediate consciousness,' nor 'presentative knowledge,' the terms by which it has been generally translated; but in view of the fact, there is no English or Western term exactly corresponding in connotation to the Sanskrit word 'Anubhava' we have adopted the term 'direct apprehension' as the nearest equivalent available.

Anubhava or Direct Apprehension is of three kinds—(1) Pramā or Right Cognition—in which a thing, horse for instance, is cognised as itself, as a horse; (2) *Apramā* or *Viparyaya,* Wrong Cognition,—as when a thing is known as what it is not; when for instance, we look upon the horse and know it as a *mule;* (3) *Samshaya,* Doubt, in which looking upon the thing, we are not certain as to whether it is what it really is, or it is something else; *f.i.* whether the horse is a horse or a mule.

Of these, the last, Doubtful Cognition, has been mentioned as a distinct topic by itself, appearing as number *three* in the opening Sūṭra. We might have reserved therefore the detailed analysis of Doubt for a future occasion, but when Gauṭama mentions it as a distinct topic, it is only by way of indicating its important bearing on argumentation. There can be no doubt that it will be best to deal with it here, as it is after all only as a form of cognition that it operates on argumentations. We shall first take up Right and Wrong Cognition; and consider these in greater detail; as on both of these, there is much diversity of opinion among the several philosophical systems.

Pramā has been defined as *ṭaṭṭvānubhūṭiḥ,*—that is, the direct definite apprehension of the thing in its real form; that is, when we know a thing as what it really is, we have the *right cognition* of it. So far all are agreed,—except of course the sceptic Vēḍānṭin, of the type of the Shrī Harṣa, the author of *Khaṇdanakhaṇdakhāḍya,* who regards the whole world as undefinable, and will not accept any definition of anything at all. The difference arises when we come to the question as to *how far* and *in what manner* the *rightness* of cognitions can be ascertained.

Four views have been held on his point as described by the *Sarvaḍarshanasaṅgraha* in the Chapter on Jaimini:—(1) The first view held by the Sāṅkhya is that validity as well as invalidity belongs to the cognition itself; neither is extraneous. (2) The second adopted by the Logician is that neither belongs to the cognition intrinsically; both are due to extraneous circumstances. (3) The third put forward by the Bauḍḍha is that invalidity belongs to the cognition intrinsically and only validity is due to extraneous circumstances. (4) The fourth accepted by the Mīmāmsaka is that intrinsically the cognition is valid; but it becomes invalid through extraneous attendant circumstances.

That both validity and invalidity are inherent in cognitions is untenable; as if cognitions were held to be inherently invalid, how could any intelligent person take up any operations in accordance with the Cognition? and if it were inherently valid, it could never be found to be wrong; while as a matter of fact, it is found in many cases, to be wrong; as in the case of the shell mistaken for silver. The same reasons also demolish the view that invalidity is inherent in cognitions and validity is extrinsic. Then there remain the two views—(1) that both validity and invalidity are extrinsic; and that validity is intrinsic and invalidity is extrinsic.

The latter view is held by the Mīmāmsakas and the older Vēḍānṭins. The older Naiyāyikas, though declaring in favour of the former view (vide. *Nyāyamañjarī*, p. 174) do not appear to be very decided against the latter. And in the final conclusion the *Nyāyamañjarī*, says that it is not particular as to validity being not inherent in Perception and the other forms of cognition; it is only with regard to verbal cognition that it cannot accept inherent validity.

According to the Mīmāmsaka cognition *per se* is valid. Any cognition that bears directly on its object is valid and true; and it is only the cognition bearing indirectly on its object that is invalid; that is to say, all direct apprehension is valid, and invalidity attaches to Remembrance only. Remembrance is invalid because it bears upon its object only indirectly, through another intervening cognition. Though every direct cognition is held to be valid, this does not preclude the possibility of *wrong* cognitions; but what the Mīmāmsaka holds is that even in the case of a wrong cognition, what vitiates it is nothing inherent in the cognition, but something wrong with other concomitant circumstances. We shall discuss this when we come to consider the nature of *Apramā* or Wrong Cognition. With regard to Cognitions Prabhakara has said—'It is strange indeed how a cognition can *apprehend* its object, and yet be *invalid*' (*Bṛīhaṭī*, Ms. p. 3). So also Kumārila—'this validity of a cognition must consist in its being an apprehension.' This view has been called the theory of the *Svaṭaḥprāmāṇya*, self-validity, of cognitions. *Pramā* can be defined as 'apprehension' only if each and every apprehension be intrinsically valid. If all cognitions were not valid, says the Mīmāmsaka, whence could we have any confidence in our own cognitions? As a matter of fact, even when it may not be found to be in agreement with the real state of things, the cognition, *as cognition* cannot but be accepted as valid; even though the thing cognised may not be there, the cognition is there all the same. If the character of being in agreement with its object were to belong to cognitions by their very nature, there the cognition would be something with a shape, each cognition having the shape of its object,—an apparent absurdity. Nor again can there be any thing or circumstance which could cause the appearance of *invalid* cognition as *valid* cognition; for what has been regarded as the cause of invalid cognition is the presence of defects in the cognitive agency; these defects being of a purely negative character, cannot have any creative force; and hence cannot produce any such positive entity as a *wrong* cognition; what they can do is to put obstacles in the way of the object being cognised in its own form; thus the wrongness due to this obstacle, would be in the cognised object, and the defects themselves would be in the causes bringing about the cognition. The objection generally brought forward against the self-evidential or self-illuminative character of Cognition is that,—inasmuch as no 'manifestation' or 'illumination' is possible, unless that which is manifested has some sort of 'form,' the 'self-illumination' of Cognition would presuppose some form for it; specially as unless each cognition has a distinctive form of its own, there could be no distinction among the cognitions themselves; and this 'form' cannot but be the same as that which belongs to the object of that cognition; as the only thing that differentiates one cognition from another is its object; and as no cognition is ever actually felt to be distinct from its object, there must be an absolute identity between the cognition and the thing cognised; and so the form of the *thing* must be the form of the cognition also. In answer to the above it is argued that if there were an absolute identity between the cognition and the thing it apprehends, then the latter could not be said to be *apprehended* by the former; the one could not be called the 'cognised' and another the 'cognition.' Nor again, is it absolutely necessary to postulate a form for cognitions, in order to serve as the basis for differentiating one cognition from another; because by the '*samvēḍana*' (Cognition or Knowledge) of a person we mean only *the manifestation of a special kind of his ḍharma or merit, which favours his active operation in connection with a certain object;* and even though this 'manifestation' or cognition, is self-illumined, that does not render its differentiation impossible; as it is called the cognition *of that object* with regard to which it favours the activity of the cogniser; and as each cognition tends to active operation in connection with a distinct object, this would afford all the basis that is necessary for its differentiation.

Then again, we must pause to consider what is meant by saying that, if the cognition were formless there could be no illumination of it. *Formlessness* certainly cannot mean *absence of character*, as even apart from its object the cognition is possessed of the *cognitional character*. Nor can any stress be laid on the fact that the cognition is devoid of such forms as the *blue* and the like. Because it is not necessary that it is only such things as are endowed with the *blue* and other forms that can be illumined? In regard to everything, it must be admitted that it is possessed of the form in which it is manifested; no other criterion is possible; and as all cognitions are manifested simply as 'cognition,' 'cognition' can be the only form that can belong to them. And the argument in favour of cognitions having the same form as their object is based upon Dreams, wherein it is argued, even though there is no real object concerned, yet the cognition that one has is in the form of some external object. Against this it is argued that, as a matter of fact, during dreams also what the cognition renders cognisable is some object of the external world; which even though not bodily present before the cogniser at that time, is yet one that has been cognised directly at some previous time, and presents itself to consciousness through impressions left upon the mind, which are aroused for the occasion. So during dreams also it is the external thing that is cognised. Says Kumārila:

'In dream-cognition also, the basis of the external object cannot be denied; in all cognitions the ultimate basis must lie in some external object,—except in certain cases, qualified by wrong connections of time and place (where alone the cognition is regarded as wrong).'

During dreams the cognition that we have must be accepted as being of the nature of Remembrance; for the simple reason that it is brought about by an arousing of existing impressions; this arousing of impressions being due to the Unseen Agency conducive to the happiness or unhappiness of the agent. It is for this reason that only that much of the previously cognised thing is *remembered,* during dreams, as would cause that happiness or unhappiness to the agent for which the Unseen Agency of this *Karma* would be ripe for operation at that moment. This also explains the fact why dream-cognition is not always of the same precise kind as an ordinary waking remembrance.

The above explanation of Dreams serves to set aside the stock argument of the Idealist—'All cognitions must be regarded as having no counterpart reality in the external world—because they are cognitions,—like Dream-Cognitions'—because as Prabhākara points out,—

'We are justified only in assuming, from a well-known effect, a cause that would make that effect possible,—and not one that would destroy it; what we find in a dream is that there is cognition of an external object; this effect can justify us in assuming—not indeed the absolute non-existence of the external object, but—the existence of the object; as without this the cognition would be an impossibility; as a general law we know it to be true that that without which something else is not possible, is the *cause* of the latter; from this it follows that the cause of Dream-cognition is some object in the external world.'

The Idealistic argument is thus found to be untenable because the corroborative instance of 'Dream-cognition' does not support of the desired conclusion; as it has been shown above that Dream-cognitions are not entirely devoid of real counterparts in the external world.

The Jaina accepts the self-validity of cognitions; but rejects its pure self-illumination. He holds cognitions to manifest themselves and also their object. As regards self-validity, the *Nyāyāvaṭāra* (verse 6) says—

न प्रत्यक्षमपि भ्रान्तम् प्रमाणात्वविनिश्चयात् ।
भ्रान्तम्प्रमाणमित्येतद् विरुद्धवचनं यत: ।

We have seen that Cognitions are *self-illumined;* the question now arises—what is meant by this 'illumination' of cognitions? The explanation given by some people is that the cognition is itself cognised by another cognition, which latter is of the nature of Sensuous Perception, brought about by the agency of the organ of 'Mind;' just in the same manner as the perceptions of pleasure and pain. This view of the perceptibility of cognition has been put forward by the Idealists; and it is thus explained by the *Ṛjuvimālā* (pp. 54-55):

'The cognition is perceptible; no perception is possible without *form* or *colour;* hence the form of *blue,* that are perceived, must belong to the cognition, and not to any external object.'

This view has been repulsed by Prabhākara and his followers. Cognitions, says Prabhākara, can never be perceptible; this is what Shabara's *Bhāṣya* means by the passage—*arṭhaviṣayā hi pratyakṣā buḍḍiḥ, na buḍḍhiviṣayā* (page 9, line 6); which means that it is the *object* that is *perceived,* and not the *cognition,*—it is not the perception that is perceived but the object. By this it is not meant that Cognition is not *cognised* or *known;* it is *cognised* certainly, but cognised only as *cognition,* not as *something cognised—samviṭṭayaiva hi samviṭ samvēḍyā na samvēḍyaṭayā,* says Prabhakara; if it were cognisable as *something cognised,* then with each individual cognition we would have to postulate Cognitions *ad infinitum.* That is to say, the Cognition, even though *cognised,* cannot itself form the *phala* (effect, object) of another act of cognition—*tasyām karma-bhāvo na yukṭah;* becasue if it were an object of another act of cognition, it would not be 'self-illumined.' We cannot regard the cognition as altogether *unknown,* as it is only when the cognition is *known* that the cognition of *things* becomes possible. What therefore we must admit is that the Cognition is something that is *self-cognised,* and has its presence known *by means of Inference;* what we apprehend by means of Inference is not any *object,* but only the *presence* of an object,—e.g., fire:—*nahyanumānāḍ rūpagrahaṇam, sanmāṭragrāhyanumānam bhavati,* says Prabhākara. So in the case in question, all the information provided by Inference is that the Cognition *is* there and not that it is *cognised;* the Inference being thus formally stated—'the Cognition exists, because we have the apprehension of its object.' In this manner, Cognition does come within the purview of Inference, which is one of the 'means of right knowledge,' and thus it is that Cognition is held to be *pramēya;* but this does not make it *samvēḍya.* Prabhākara draws a subtle distinction between '*pramēya*' and '*samvēḍya;*' the '*samvēḍya*' is that where the form or shape of the object is manifested and apprehended; and this can occur only in the case of objects perceived by the senses; in the case of '*pramēya*' on the other hand, it is not necessary for it to have a form or shape; cognition cannot be '*samvēḍya,*' (and hence also it cannot be *perceptible);* but as having its presence apprehended by means of Inference,—which is one of the '*pramāṇas,*'—it has to be regarded as '*pramēya.*'

The above view has beed accepted, to a certain extent, by Kamārila and his followers also. The *Shāṣṭraḍīpika* (p. 37) explains:—(1) that the Perception, of a certain thing ends, not in a further cognition of that perception, but in the *āparokṣya* or *prakataṭā, direct apprehensibility,* of that thing; and (2) that every act of Perception involves a certain relationship between the *perceiver* and the *perceived,*—the former being the agent, and the latter the object of that act; this agent-and-object relationship is not possible without some activity on the part of the agent; hence the presence of this relationship leads to the inference of its invariable concomitant,—*viz.*, the action of the agent; and it is this *action* that, in the case of Knowledge, is known as 'cognition;' and it has been shown to be *inferable* from the relationship between the cognising self and the cognised object *'Mānasapratyakṣagamyorṭhēna sahāṭmanaḥ sambanḍho jñānaṅkalpayaṭīti ramaṇīyam,* says the *Shāsṭraḍīpikā* (pp. 37-38). The *Shabara Bhāṣya* (1.1.5)—'One is not cognisant of the cognition until the object has been cognised; when the object is cognised, this fact leads to the inference of the cognition; from the effect, in the shape of the manifestation of the object to consciousness, we infer the cause, in the shape of the cognition.'

The Naiyāyika, intent upon the Veda being regarded as the word of God, denies the self-validity of cognitions, specially verbal; we have seen that the older Naiyāyika, even though demolishing the self-validity of cognitions, is not keen about other forms of cognition except the verbal; but later Naiyāyikas have taken up a decided attitude against the self-validity of all cognitions. And here is what the *Ṭarkabhāṣa,* a work of the 14th Century, says on the point:

"In connection with the Instruments of Right Cognition we proceed to consider the following: In most cases, when the man has cognised the water, and has assured himself of the validity of his cognition, he proceeds to take up the water; but in some cases, the mere suspicion or doubtful knowledge of the presence of water leads the man to proceed to take up the water; and it is only after he has found the water to be actually present that he becomes assured of the validity of his original cognition. Such are the facts; and upon these some people opine as follows: 'In all cases, the man proceeds to activity after having previously ascertained the validity of his cognition; inasmuch as the validity of cognitions is self-evident and self-assured. That is to say, whenever a man has a certain cognition, at the same time, he also recognises the validity of that cognition; the apprehender of the validity of the cognition not being different from the apprehender of the cognition itself; and it is this *independence of any apprehender other than that of the cognition itself* that constitutes the 'self-sufficiency' of the validity of the cognition. There is no doubt that the cognition itself is apprehended before the activity; as if it were not so, wherefore could there arise any doubt as to its validity or otherwise? For certainly, until the object of doubt has been cognised, the doubt cannot arise. Thus then, the Cognition itself being already apprehended by the instrumentality of Presumption based upon the impossibility of its *apprehendedness* (except on such apprehension), the validity of that cognition comes to be apprehended by means of Presumption; and thereupon follows the action of the man. And it is not true that at first the cognition alone is apprehended; and its validity is apprehended only after the resultant activity of the man has led to his attaining the object of that cognition.'

"In answer to the above, we argue as follows: We do not admit that the cognition is apprehended by the instrumentality of the presumption based upon the impossibility of its *apprehendedness* (except on such apprehension), as has been declared above; we are all the further away from admitting that the validity is also apprehended by Presumption. To explain;—what our opponent means may be stated thus: As soon as one has the cognition of the jar, there is recognised the *apprehendedness* of the cognition, in the notion expressed in the words 'the jar is cognised by me;' and from this it is inferred that when the cognition is produced, there is produced in it a certain property in the shape of *apprehendedness;* inasmuch as this *apprehendedness* had not been produced before the cognition,—and is produced upon the production or appearance of the cognition;—the natural conclusion pointed to by these positive and negative premises is that 'the *apprehendedness* is produced by the cognition;' and thus the property named *apprehendedness* produced by cognition is not possible without the cognition,—the appearance of the effect being not possible without the cause; and by means of the Presumption based upon this, the *apprehendedness* indicates its own cause or source, in the shape of the Cognition. This we hold, is not right; because *apprehendedness* is nothing apart from the character of being the object of the Cognition.

"The Opponent retorts—'The jar is said to be the object of cognition only in virtue of its being the substratum of the *apprehendedness* produced by the Cognition. Because the said *objectivity* (of the jar) cannot be of the nature of identity; no identity being possible between the jar and the cognition, of which one is the object (*viṣaya*) and the other the subject (*viṣayin*). If the 'objectivity' consisted in the fact of the cognition being produced from (or proceeding from) it, then that objectivity would belong to the sense-organs and such other sources from which cognition is produced. This leads us to the inference that by the cognition there has been produced in the jar something whereby that jar alone, and nothing else, becomes the *object* of that cognition; and this something is what we call *apprehendedness.* It is in this manner that the *apprehendedness* is proved, not only by direct sense-perception, but also by presumption based upon the impossibility of the said *objectivity.*'

"This is not right, we reply. Because, as a matter of fact, the *objective* and *subjective* characters proceed from the very nature of things; that is to say, there is a natural peculiarity in the object and its cognition, by virtue of which one is the *object* and the other the *subject* in relation to the other. If this were not so, then no objectivity could belong to past and future things; as it is not possible for any *apprehendedness* being produced in these by cognition; inasmuch as it is not possible for a property to be produced in an object that does not exist at the time (and *apprehendedness* is only a property). Then again, inasmuch as the *apprehendedness* also, in its time, would be the object of its own cognition, that would necessitate the assumption of another *apprehendedness;* and thus there would be no end to the number of *apprehendednesses,*—thus assumed. If, in order to avoid this, this objectivity of the *apprehendedness* were held to be something inborn in itself, independent of any further *apprehendedness* then the same might be admitted with regard to the jar and such other things also; what then would be the necessity of assuming any *apprehendedness* at all? If (for the sake of argument) we admit of such a thing as *apprehendedness;* even in that case, the cognition would be indicated by mere *apprehendedness* in general; while its validity would be indicated by a particular form of apprehendedness,—that form which is in consonance with the cognition of the instrument of right cognition; and such being the case, how can the validity of the cognition be held to be apprehended by the apprehender of the cognition itself? If there were some such peculiar *apprehendedness,* in consonance with the cognition of the instrument of right cognition, by which the cognition and its validity were both apprehended simultaneously;—then the same might be said with regard to *invalidity* also; namely that there is some such peculiar *apprehendedness* in consonance with the cognition of the instrument of invalid cognition, by virtue of which this cognition and its *invalidity* are both apprehended simultaneously; and thus the invalidity of the cognition also might be regarded as self-evidenced. If, even in face of this, the *invalidity* of the cognition be held to be due to extraneous circumstances, then its *validity* also would be due to extraneous circumstances,—that is to say, apprehended by means other than that which apprehends the cognition. It is for these reasons that we hold that the cognition is apprehended by Sense-perception obtained through the agency of the mind, while its validity is apprehended by means of Inference; for instance, when the man seeking for water has the cognition (or perception) of water, the exertion that he puts forth is either *fruitful* or not fruitful; of these the fruitful exertion is called '*samartha*' or 'fit,' 'capable;' and it is through the fruitfulness of the exertion that the validity of the cognition (exciting this exertion) is *inferred;* the inferential syllogism appearing in the following form—'the cognition of water in question is valid, because it gives rise to fruitful exertion,—that which is not valid never gives rise to fruitful exertion,—as for example the invalid cognition;'—this is based on the universal negative premiss 'that which is not valid never gives rise to fruitful exertion;' the 'subject' of the syllogism is *that cognition of water which gives rise to fruitful exertion;* and the *'probandum'* is the *validity* of that cognition. What is meant by the 'validity' (prāmāṇya) of the cognition in this case is the fact of its being in due consonance with its real object,—and not the character of being the instrument of right cognition; as if it meant the latter, then the syllogism would become fallacious; in view of Remembrance, which while giving rise to fruitful exertion, and thus fulfilling the condition of the *probans, is not* the instrument of right cognition, and thus fails in reference to the *probandum.* The *probans* of the syllogism is the 'character of giving rise to fruitful exertion.' The validity of the cognition, after it has become rightly effective (by giving rise to fruitful exertion), being thus ascertained by means of the above Inference, we are led to infer, on the strength of the analogy of this cognition of water, the validity of similar cognitions of water, even before they have given rise to any exertion, and thereby proved themselves to be rightly effective,—this inference being based upon the fact of these latter cognitions being similar on all points to the previous cognition; and this inference is based upon negative and positive premisses. Thus then, we conclude that the validity of cognitions is apprehended by means other than those whereby the cognitions themselves are apprehended."

According to the *Prāmāṇyavāḍa (Ṭaṭtvachinṭāmaṇi,* p. 198), the validity and invalidity of cognitions are both cognised by means of Inference. If every cognition were self-valid, it argues, we would have no doubts regarding the validity of any cognition; while as a matter of fact, we have such doubts in many cases. When we see a horse, the first cognition that we have is in the form 'this is a horse;' this is followed by a vague undefined idea in the form 'I have seen a horse;' and when I actually feel and touch the horse, I argue—'the cognition I have had must be *valid,* or else I would not have actually found the horse where I perceived it.' Thus that the cognition is *valid* is ascertained by Inference.

There is difference among philosophers, not only on the self-validity of cognitions; but also with regard to the exact nature of the apprehension of the cognition itself. We have seen that the Mīmāmsaka regards it as beyond Perception, known only by means of Inference; while the Naiyāyika regards it as known by Perception. The Vēḍānṭin, along with all other Idealists, holds it to be '*svaprakāsha,*' 'self-illumined,' this being the natural corrollary to the Idealistic standpoint, according to which there *is* nothing else except *Idea,* and ultimately, every cognition must depend upon itself. Thus then, according to these, what is manifested in the cognition is the cognition itself; according to the Naiyāyika, the cognition manifests, or renders cognised, something else; the Jainas hold *(Nyāyāvaṭāra-vivṛiṭi,* p. 4) that the cognition makes comprehended both itself and something else, *i.e.* the object. This Jaina work on Logic, refutes the absolute self-illumination of cognitions by the argument that if there is no *object to be cognised,* no *cognition* would be possible; and it meets the Naiyāyika by arguing that what does not manifest itself cannot manifest anything at all; and it defines Pramāṇa as सकलप्रतिभासस्य समस्तसंवेदनस्य भ्रान्तत्वासिद्धितो विपर्यस्तत्वानिष्पत्तेः यत् स्फुटं स्वान्यनिश्चायि सुनिश्चिततया स्वपरप्रकाशकं तत् प्रमाणाम् (Vvṛīṭi on Verse 7). That is, 'As it is not possible for all cognitional phenomena to be invalid, Pramāṇa is that which clearly manifests itself and other things and brings conviction, to oneself as well as to others.'

Wrong Cognition

We have seen what is Pramā, Right Cognition, and also what is Pramāṇa, the Instrument of Right Cognition. We proceed to analyse Bhrānṭi, *Wrong Cognition.*

There is a difference of opinion among the various philosophies as to the exact nature of Wrong Cognition, as indicated by Vāchaspaṭi Mishra in his Ṭaṭparya-Tīkā, pp. 53-54. The names given to the several views are as follow:

(1) *Asaṭkhyāṭivāḍa:* The theory of the apprehension of what has no existence, held by the Bauḍḍha-Nihilist.

(2) *Āṭmakhyāṭivāḍa:* The theory of Self-apprehension, held by the Bauḍḍha-Idealist.

(3) *Anirvachanīyakhyāṭivāḍa:* The theory of Inexplicable Apprehension, held by the Vēḍānṭin.

(4) *Akhyāṭivāḍa*: The theory of Non-apprehension, held by the Mīmāmsaka.

(5) *Anyaṭhākhyāṭivāḍa*: The theory of Disssembling Apprehension, held by the Naiyāyika.

We shall deal in detail with this controversy; as it is extremely interesting.

(1) *Asaṭkhyāṭi* of The Bauḍḍha Nihilist

I have not yet had access to any Bauḍḍha work giving us first-hand information as to what is meant by their *Asaṭkhyāṭi* theory. But from the Tātparya-Tīkā (p. 54) of Vāchaspaṭi Mishra, who appears to have had access to the work of the great Bauḍḍha logician, Diṅnāga, we can glean the following account of the theory:

We become sure of a certain cognition being *wrong* only when that cognition is followed by another cognition which contravenes this former. For instance, when we see a bright thing, and know it as silver, this knowledge can be regarded as wrong only when subsequently we have some such cognition as 'this is *not* silver, this is a piece of shell.' Thus then, on the strength of this later sublating cognition, the only right view to take of the nature of Wrong Cognition is that it manifests or makes known, something that is *asaṭ,* that does not exist: the worng cognition of silver affords us the knowledge of silver that does not exist. What is apprehended by the cognition is *silver,* and this *silver,* at that particular time and place, has no existence, is *asaṭ*. It has been argued against this view that it requires a certain potency in the thing to enable it to form the object of a cognition; and that which has no existence, which does not exist,–it is not possible for such a non-entity to be endowed with any potency; how then can it form the object of any cognition? The answer given by the Bauḍḍha Nihilist is that it is not impossible for a non-existent thing to form the object of a cognition. This would be impossible only if for being such an object it were necessary for the thing to be endowed with some sort of causal potency; as a matter of fact, the potency required is not necessarily the causal one; all that is necessary is some sort of potency or capability in the cognition concerned; and there is nothing inherently impossible in the cognition having the capability of rendering apprehended things existent as well as non-existent; it is not necessary for this that there should be some potency in the thing itself; it is sufficient if the Cognition is equipped with such a potency; and the Cognition is not a non-entity. Thus then, the conclusion is that it is this capability of rendering apprehended things not existent that distinguishes the *wrong* from the *right* cognition.

The Naiyāyika's objection against this view is thus put forth:

Does this mean that what is apprehended by Wrong Cognition is an absolute non-entity, something that has no existence at all? or that it is a thing that exists, but only at some other place and time? If it is the latter, then this theory does not differ from the *Anyaṭhākhyāṭi* view: for as thus interpreted, the meaning of *Asaṭkhyāṭi* is that it represents, makes apprehended, the thing as *existing* at a time and place where it is *non-existing; i.e.* represents a real thing as of a different character from what it actually is; and this does not mean that what is apprehended is a non-entity. If the object of Wrong Cognition were held to be an absolute non-entity,—even then, in the first place it would be difficult to explain how an absolute non-entity can form the object of cognition; and secondly, even in this case if we analyse the wrong cognition, it comes to this that it represents a thing as an entity, as existing, when in reality it is a non-entity, non-existent; and this also is the same as representing the thing as what it is not; and this is '*Anyaṭhākhyāṭi,*' not '*Asaṭkhyāṭi.*'

It may be noted here that the Nihilist, even though perhaps agreeing in the main with this presentment of Wrong Cognition, has chosen to call his view '*Asaṭkhyāṭi;*' as under his theory everything is a non-entity; the 'void' or *Shūnya* being the only entity, if it can be called an *entity,* that he posits.

(2) The *Āṭmakhyāṭivāḍa* of The Bauḍḍha Idealist

The Bauḍḍha Idealist does not accept the *Asaṭkhyāṭi* view, as he finds it necessary to express everything in terms of 'Idea' which is the only entity that he posits. By this view, says Vāchaspaṭi Mishra (*Ṭāṭ.*, p. 53), in Wrong Cognition what happens, and what makes the cognition *wrong*, is that the Cognition or Idea–which has a purely internal existence, in the mind of the cogniser–presents *itself* as a thing having an *external* existence; so that by this view, the cognition of all *external* things is wrong; and the logical outcome of this view of Wrong Cognition is that the entire external world is unreal; because the very conception of externality involves the presenting of the Idea as something *external;* 'not accepting the reality of any external thing, the Idealist has held that, in any cognition of external things as such, the cognition turns upon and presents itself'–says the Jaina wirter, Siḍḍhasēna-Ḍivākara, in his *Nyāyāvaṭāra* (p. 4.)

This theory is worked out in greater detail in the *Vivaraṇapramēyasaṅgraha* (Trans. p. 85 et. seq., *Indian Thought,* Vol. I, 271)–In the case of the wrong cognition of silver, the silver must be regarded as of the nature of an idea, the Idealist argues; since it is something immediately presented to the mind, without any contact of the sense-organ with the object; and the cognition *of silver,* under the circumstances, proceeds on the basis of a mental impression: by the impression, from which the idea of silver originates, we understand a previous cognition of silver which, at some time or other, had arisen in the beginningless series of cognitions; such an impression produces, at some time, an idea of the same kind as itself, although many ideas of a different kind may intervene between the impression and the idea; the case is analogous to that of a grain of wheat which in the end gives rise to another grain of the same kind, although the sprout and several other effects of a different kind intervene between the grain sown and the second grain harvested out of it. As regards the case of the wrong cognition of silver, we may define the impression that gives rise to the cognition, as the series of ideas which were produced by the previous idea of silver; this previous idea again was, in its turn, produced by a yet earlier idea. What really exists is, therefore, only an idea having the form or character of silver, which is the result of a beginningless series of impressions; it is this idea that appears to consciousness as something *external*; and herein lies the erroneousness of the cognition.

The Naiyāyika's objection to this Idealistic view is that everything being Idea, the cognition, the cogniser and the cognised object,—each of these is mere Idea; so that if in the cognition of the silver what appeared to consciousness was only the Idea itself, then the cognition would be in the form '*I am silver*'—and not as '*this* is silver.' In addition to this, this view, involving as it does the denial of the reality of the entire external world, is open to all the objections to which such a denial is open. Lastly, under this view also, the silver, which, as Idea, has a purely internal existence, is cognised as external; that is, it is cognised as what it is not; and so far as this is concerned, this is included in the Nyāya view of '*Anyaṭhākhyāṭi,*' which is free from the vitiating taint of the absurdities that are involved in the Idealistic way of presenting the case.

The Idealistic Bauḍḍha view has been severely criticised by the *Vivaraṇaprамēyasaṅgraha* also (I. Th. I, p. 273)—Is that silver, the Vēḍāntin asks, which appears in the shell, on account of its extraordinary nature, devoid of origination? or does it originate as ordinary silver does? On the former view it would not be of the nature of a rising cognition, which it actually is. On the second view, it must originate either from a cognition or from a thing. The latter alternative is excluded, since the Bauḍḍhas do not admit the existence of external things. On the former alternative it cannot be pure cognition that originates the idea of silver; for pure cognition constitutes final release. If, on the other hand, what originates the silver is a cognition (not pure, but) itself due to a vitiated cause, is it that same originating cognition which apprehends the silver? or is it a cognition other than that? The former alternative is not possible; for since the originating and the originated cognitions are both 'momentary,' and hence occupy different moments of time, the consciousness of immediately presented silver would thus not come about at all. If, in the second place, it is another cognition that apprehends the silver, it cannot be a cognition produced by a non-vitiated cause; for this would be too wide an assumption; inasmuch as there would be no reason why such a cognition should specially apprehend silver. If, on the other hand, the cognition which apprehends the silver is produced by a *vitiated* cause, that cause is either silver or it is not silver. In the former case, you ascribe to silver causal efficiency; and this means that the cause *is*, has *being*; you thus acknowledge the silver as a real *external* thing. If the cause is not silver, silver cannot be the object of cognition; for you yourself admit that that object is the cause which imparts its form to, and determines the precise form of, cognition. It is thus evident that on the *Āṭmakhyāṭi* view, the cognition of silver could not come about at all.

(3) *Anirvachanīya-Khyāṭi* of the Veḍānṭin

The Vēḍānṭa view of the Wrong Cognition of silver is that the cognition of silver in this case is neither a *remembrance* nor a *direct apprehension;* and yet the presentation of the silver to consciousness may be explained in the following manner: In the first place the sense-organ—which, on the occasion of what has been called erroneous cognition, must be held to be impaired by a certain defect—coming into contact with the shell, gives rise to a certain modification of the internal organ, which thereupon assumes merely the form of a *this;* which is inevitable so long as the thing is not actually known as what it is;—next, Consciousness reveals itself with regard to this *this-ness,* and the modification of the internal organ which apprehends it; at the same time, that part of General Nescience, which has for its locus the Consciousness as manifested or determined in the manner described, is thrown into a state of agitation, owing to the influence of the defect, which, in all cases of error, must be present;–on being thus agitated, that Nescience, which has for its locus the Consciousness determined by the *this*-element, owing to the assistance which it receives from impression left behind by previously perceived silver–which impression, on the present occasion, is resuscitated by similarity between silver and the glittering shell before the eyes,–illusorily manifests itself in the form of silver; that Nescience, on the other hand, which has for its locus the Consciousness as defined by the function of the internal organ, being assisted by the impression left behind by the original function by which silver was apprehended in the past, illusorily modifies itself into the form of that function;–finally these two illusory modifications or projections of Nescience–namely, that of silver and that of the function–are irradiated by witnessing Consciousness, which constitutes their substrate; and thereby there arises the cognition of silver. There indeed really are two cognitions–the function of the internal organ, and the function of the nescience; but the object of the two become one, in so far as the real and the unreal element (*i.e.,* the *this* and the *silver,* respectively) mutually identify themselves; and as hence the result determined by the object (*i.e.,* the cognition) also becomes one, the cognition may be regarded as *one* in a figurative sense. Although no doubt the contact of the sense-organ with the object and the mental impression left behind by previous apprehension are capable of giving rise, independently of each other, to true direct cognition, on the one, and to remembrance, on the other hand,–yet the mere origination, in immediate succession, of direct true cognition and of remembrance would not result in activity,–such for instance as the attempt to take possession of the presumed silver; hence it becomes necessary to assume a *single* false cognition, resulting from present sense-contact and mental impression combined. Nor need there be anything incongruous in a *single* cognition proceeding from a multiplicity of causes; as this is found to be the case with wrong inferential cognition; every one of these proceeds from a perception as assisted by a number of remembrances and impressions. Nor again is it contrary to reason to maintain the non-reality of silver, when it is cognised as real;—as what we maintain is that in the case in question there is connection of the real existence of the shell with the imaginary silver; and even though this connection is cognised as real, yet it is not irrational to regard it as unreal; for *existence* or *being* is of three different kinds—(1) real existence, which belongs to Brahman only; (2) empirical existence, which is conditioned by Māyā or Illusion, and belongs to fire, water and such other so-called real things of ordinary normal experience; and (3) apparent existence, which is conditioned by Nescience, and belongs to the silver as presumed in the shell. Of these three, if the two latter are called 'unreal' or 'false,' there need be nothing irrational in this; as mere *empirical* or *apparent* existence cannot be regarded as 'real,' in the true sense of the word. Nor is this hypothesis of such falseness devoid of proof; for the subsequent judgment 'silver *falsely* appeared to me' expresses the recognition of the unreality of the silver and its cognition. The general conclusion therefrom is that in the erroneous cognition of silver, the silver is the product of Māyā or Illusion. And as Māyā is something the exact nature and properties of which cannot be determined or explained, this hypothesis has been called '*Anirvachanīyakhyāṭi.*' (I. Th. I, p. 274.)

The difference between the Āṭmakhyāṭi of the Bauḍḍha and the Anirvachanīyakhyāṭi of the Vēḍānṭin Idealist appears to be that by the former hypothesis, the form of the cognised silver is imposed on the cognition, while according to the latter it is imposed on the modification or function of the internal organ.

(4) *Ākhyātivāda*—The Theory of 'Non-Apprehension' Held by the Mīmāmsaka

The Mīmāmsaka lays stress on *all* cognitions being regarded as *valid*; and in view of this he supplies the following explanation of wrong and doubtful cognitions: In the case of all cognitions, the *object* of cognition is that same thing which is presented to consciousness by it; and in the stock-example of Wrong Cognition—'this is silver'—what is presented to consciousness being *silver*, it cannot be denied that *silver* is the *object* of the cognition, and not *shell*, which latter does not enter into the cognition at all; for this reason the judgment in question cannot be said to fulfil the conditions of 'wrong cognition,'—which has been defined as 'the cognition of a thing in something that is not that thing;' for in the case in question, it is not the *shell* that is cognised *as silver*; as a matter of fact, the *shell* is not cognised at all; what is cognised is the *silver*. This sounds rather subtle; but its truth cannot be denied; to say that it is the *shell* that is cognised would not be true to fact. What happens in the case in that, though the object present before the eye is the shell, yet, inasmuch as the perceiver fails to notice the distinctive features peculiar to the shell, and notices only those features that are common to the shell and the silver, he fails to apprehend the difference between the two things; and this gives rise to his cognition of *silver*,—this cognition thus being due to the *non-apprehension* of the difference between *silver* and the *object before the eyes*. The idea of silver also comes to his mind by the force of memory, which is aroused by the perception of the properties common to the shell and the silver; though the silver is remembered, it is not remembered as 'that'—something perceived in the past—which would have sufficed to differentiate that '*that* silver' of the past from the '*this* thing' of the present, before the eyes,—the non-perception of 'that' being due to a certain weakness of the mind; thus then, the apprehension of *silver* in the judgment 'this is silver' cannot but be regarded as an act of memory. This silver not being actually before the eyes, cannot be regarded as *perceived*; nor are there any factors available sufficient to bring about the *inferential* or any other kind of cognition of it. Though the judgment in question is thus found to partake of the dual character of *remembrance* and *direct apprehension,* and, as such differs from the ordinary *valid* cognition of silver, (which is wholly *apprehension*),—yet, in actual experience, it is not cognised as so different; and this for the simple reason that,—just as in the case of real silver the *thing perceived,* is not cognised as different from 'silver,' so in the case in question also. Thus in actual experience, there is found to be no difference between the 'right' and the 'wrong' cognition of silver; specially as both equally give rise to the same kind of activity on the part of the agent: in both cases he stoops to pick up the thing.

The above is the statement of the Mīmāmsaka position by Prabhākara. The view held by Kumārila does not differ materially from this. In so far as the judgment 'this is silver' involves a cognition *per se,* it is valid; it is quite valid for the cogniser at the time that he has the cognition; that it is sublated or rejected by subsequent experience is another matter. The subsequent experience must be regarded as destroying the validity that belonged to the cognition as *something cognised,* and not *as cognition* as such. Says the *Shāsṭraḍīpikā:*

> *Ṭasmāṭ svaṭaḥ-prāmāṇyam prāpṭam arṭhānyaṭhāṭva-kāraṇaḍoṣa-jñānābhyamapoḍyaṭē, iṭyavashyamañgikarṭavyam.* (p. 15, l. 16) and again on p. 31, L. 5:

> *Yaṭra prayaṭnēnānviṣyamāṇe kāraṇaḍoṣo bāḍkakajñānam vā nopalabhyaṭē ṭaṭ pramāṇam, iṭarachchāpramāṇam.*

The various stock-examples of wrong cognition are thus explained by the *Mīmāmsaka*: In the case of the white conch-shell being perceived as *yellow,* what happens is this: There is a *real* yellowness that is perceived, that belonging to the bile affecting the eye; the whiteness of the conch fails to be noticed on account of the disease in the eye; so what is perceived on the one hand, is the conch alone, without any colour; and on the other, the yellowness without the object to which it belongs; thus a colourless object and objectless colour having been perceived at the same time, what more natural than that the two perceptions should coalesce, and present to consciousness the two combined, the *yellow conch*? Even when the man picks up the conch-shell, and look at it more closely, he still sees it as yellow; and thus in this case there is nothing that could make the cognition *wrong*: in fact, so far as the man himself is concerned, he can regard the cognition as wrong, only when he knows of the disease in his eye—the *Kāraṇadoṣa* of the *Shāstradīpikā*. In the same manner, when a person suffering from bile feels sugar to be bitter, what happens is that he fails to taste the sweetness of the sugar, which he feels to be tasteless; but he feels the bitterness of the bile brought into the mouth; and the two coalescing, present to his consciousness the *bitter sugar*. In the case of a person seeing two moons, the rays of light issue from the two eyes, at two different times; and it is natural that two images of the moon are imprinted on the retina, and thence presented to the man's consciousness. In all cases of vision, there must be two such images; but in the normal condition of the eyes, the interval between the issuing forth of the visual light from the two eyes is too subtle; hence the two images are found to coalesce and give rise to the perception of the thing as one only. And when there is some defect in the eyes whereby the interval between the two is enhanced, the two images appear as distinct, and give rise to the notion of *two moons*. When we mistake one direction for the other, the real direction is not seen; and the name of the other direction is remembered; and what is actually seen and what is remembered, coalesce, and give rise to the cognition of the two combined. So here the mistake lies in the *remembered* name and not in the *apprehension.* Lastly, as regards Dreams, the things presented to consciousness are only *remembered;* and yet they appear as if they were actually *apprehended* at the time; and what happens is that the factor of *having been apprehended at some previous time* is lost sight of, and it is this factor only that differentiates what is remembered from what is *apprehended.* As regards the force that energises or excites the impression which brings about the remembrance, this, it is held, is supplied by that Unseen Agency which guides the percipient or dreaming Souls during their earthly sojourn. If the time at which the man is sleeping is one at which he is destined to experience pleasure, the Unseen Agency of his destiny awakens those impressions that bring to his mind pleasant memories; and similarly if he is destined to experience pain at the time, there arise those impressions that bring unpleasant memories. This accounts for the fact that dreams are sometimes pleasant, and sometimes unpleasant; this pleasure or pain, so far as the actual *feeling* is concerned, is as real as any that is experienced during waking consciousness. This view of Dreams is thus supported by the *Shāsṭraḍīpikā* (p. 39, 1.10): 'In dreams also, what is cognised is the external object perceived elsewhere in the past and presented to consciousness during sleep by an Unseen Agency; the cognition itself is quite valid, so far as the objet is concerned; the wrongness or invalidity comes in only when it is regarded as something actually *apprehended at the time;* and not as only *remembered;* and the cause of this lies in such discrepancies as are due to sleep; thus the invalidity pertains to the accessory details, and not to the cognition *per se.*' From all this it is abundantly clear, that wherever we have actual apprehension, there is nothing wrong, and that the mistake comes in only when some factor of remembrance crops into the Cognition. And what differentiates these Cognitions from the right Cognition is the fact that in these former there is *non-apprehension,* either actually of the thing concerned, or of the difference between what is seen and what is remembered; and on this account, the view has been called the view of 'Non-apprehension', '*Akhyāṭī*'. (I. Th. II, pp. 148-152.)

It is interesting to note that the Jaina philosophers appear to favour this Mīmāmsaka view of Wrong Cognition. Siḍḍhasēna-Ḍivākara, the great Jaina logician, says in his *Nyāyāvaṭāra:*

'Perception is never wrong; as it is always recognised as valid; to speak of it as valid and at the same time, as wrong would be a contradiction in terms? (Verse 4) and so also inference (Verse 5).'

'Wrong Cognition is not possible,' adds the Commentary, 'because it is absolutely impossible for a Cognition that apprehends an entire object to be wrong, as valid cognition, Pramāṇa, has been defined as that which is clear and distinct, bringing conviction to oneself as well as to others, which presents to consciousness itself as well as its object; and all these conditions are fulfilled by the so-called Wrong Cognition, at least at the time that it appears.'

(5) The *Anyahāṭkhyāṭi* or Theory of Dissembling Cognition, Held by the Naiyāyika

The *Nyāyamañjarī* (pp. 180-83,) traverses in detail the position of the Mīmāmsāka; and so does the *Tāṭparyatikā* on p. 57. But before we proceed with the later works we should begin with what the earliest Nyāya works have got to say with regard to the nature of Wrong Cognition.

Here is what the Vāṭsyāyana-Bhāṣya says on the subject under Su. 1-1-2: 'Of Wrong Notion mentioned in the Sūṭra as the first to cease after the attainment of true knowledge, there are various kinds, pertaining as it does to the several objects of cognition, beginning with Soul and ending with

Final Release. With reference to the Soul the wrong notion is in the form, 'there is no such thing as Soul;' with regard to the non-soul, people have a wrong notion when it is regarded as the Soul;' when pain is regarded as pleasure, we have the wrong notion of pain; and so on when the non-eternal is regarded as eternal; when non-safety is regarded as safety; when the fearful is regarded as fearless; when the disgusting is regarded as agreeable; when that which deserves to be discarded is regarded as worthy of not being discarded; when with regard to activity, we have such notions as 'there is no such thing as Karma, nor any result of Karma'; when with regard to defects we have the notion that 'Metempsychosis is not due to defects;' with regard to birth and death, we have such wrong notions as 'there is no such thing as a living being, or a being with Soul, who could die, or having died, could be born again,' 'the transmigration of living beings is without cause,' 'the cessation of birth is without cause,' 'transmigration has a beginning, but no end,' 'even though caused, transmigration is not caused by Karma,' 'transmigration can have no relation to the Soul, as it consists only in the disruption, at death, and restoration, at rebirth, of the continuous connection of such things as the body, the sense-organs, the intellect and the sensations;' with regard to Final Release, we have such wrong notions as 'it is something terrible, involving as it does the cessation of all activity,' 'in final release, which consists in separation from all things, we lose much that is desirable,' 'how can any intelligent person have any longing for Final Release, in which there is neither pleasure nor pain, nor any sensation at all?'

From the above detailed account of Wrong Cognition, the *Vārṭika* has deduced the definition that 'Wrong Cognition is the cognition of a thing as what it is not,—the apprehending of a thing in what is not that thing,'—*Aṭasmin ṭaḍiti jñānam.* And this is the definition that has been accepted by all later logicians. The *Taṭṭvachinṭāmaṇi* also accepts the same definition, only expressing it in a form more in keeping with the precise terminology invented by itself. The definition as propounded by it is तदभाववति तत्प्रकारकं ज्ञानम्—'when where there is non-existence of a certain thing, there is a cognition qualified or objectified by that thing, that cognition is *wrong*.' (*Taṭṭvachinṭāmaṇi,* p. 401). In the proper style of the Neo-logician, this definition is on p. 418 further improved into the elaborate form—स्वसमानाधिकरणप्रकारानवच्छिन्नविषयताप्रतियोगि ज्ञानम, which, translated literally, means—'the Cognition that has for its objective counterpart a thing that is not characterised by properties actually co-existent with itself;'—which comes to the same thing as 'the cognition of a thing as what it is not.'

The Nāiyāyika view is given in clear great detail in the *Nyāyamañjarī* (pp. 180-83):

It has been held by many philosophers that the Wrong Cognition 'this is silver' involves the direct apprehension of 'this' and the remembrance of 'silver;' and the mistake lies in these not being properly discriminated and being allowed to coalesce. This analysis of the cognition cannot be accepted; as, like Recognition, the cognition of silver is always known as one only; the cognition being in the form: 'This substance that is lying before me, possessed of whiteness brightness and such other properties, is the particular thing called *silver;'* and in this cognition the silver appears as something that *is being known* at the time, and not as something that *has been known* in the past; and in remembrance, the object always appears as something that *has been known.* So the notion of silver in the case of the wrong cognition of silver cannot be regarded as remembrance. Then again, the Mīmāmsaka regarding all cognitions as self-illumined,—how can he justify his regarding one part of the cognition (of the wrong cognition of silver) as 'direct apprehension,' and another as 'remembrance'? It has been held that the notion of 'this' in the cognition 'this is silver' is direct apprehension; now let us consider what is it that, really appears in the cognition of 'this'? If the 'this' herein cognised is the piece of shell along with all its peculiarities, then how could its perception, in any way lead to the remembrance of silver? Even if such remembrance were possible through the similarity of the shell to the silver, this could not account for that non-discrimination, or identification, of the two which we find in the cognition 'this is silver;' when we see a man, and are reminded of another man resembling him, this does not lead us to identify the two men. The only rational explanation of the cognition 'this is silver' is to regard it as due to the remembrance of the particular thing silver,—this remembrance of the thing, not before the eyes, being brought about by the perception of properties common to the two things, as aided by the arousing of the impression of the other thing (silver) left on the mind; hence the 'this' refers not to the shell, but in a general way to the 'thing possessed of the properties of whiteness and the rest;' and through the aforesaid remembrance, this general thing, instead of being particularised as 'shell,' comes to be particularised as 'silver;' and it is because the observer knows that he is actually apprehending the silver that, being desirous of having silver, he stoops to pick it up; until he knows that what he is seeing is actually silver he cannot stoop to pick it up. Hence it must be admitted that in the Wrong Cognition, we have the direct apprehension of silver, and not only the obliteration of the fact of its being only remembered. And the direct apprehension of silver is brought about by the instrumentality of the sense-organ, so far vitiated by some defect that it is incapable of apprehending at the time those peculiar features of the object that distinguish it from other similar things, and apprehends only those properties that are common to both; and this apprehension is further assisted by the remembrance, through association, of the features peculiar to the other thing (silver). When we speak of the organ being defective in this case, it is only in reference to the true cognition; so far as the bringing about of the Wrong Cognition itself is concerned, the organ is fully efficient. Then again, we are all agreed as to the fact that the wrong cognition 'this is silver' is sublated by the subsequent apprehension 'this is not silver;' and on being analysed this sublating cognition comes to mean this—'what I had seen was not silver;' and this must mean that the silver had been *seen*, and not only *remembered*; as in the latter case the sublating cognition should have been 'what I had *remembered* is not silver.'

As regards the substratum of the wrong cognition of silver,—in the first place, the silver itself may be regarded as that substratum; though the silver is not present, yet there need be nothing objectionable in regarding the cognition as having its substrate in the silver recalled to the mind; what has come to the mind can be the substratum of cognition, which is a mental process. In case this be not acceptable, we can have as substratum the shell, which has its own form obscured, and has taken for the nonce the form of the other thing (silver). These two views are only tentatively put forward; the real view held by the logician is that the substratum consists only of the entity that is vaguely known at the time as 'this object,' without its peculiarities being definitely ascertained.

According to the Vēḍānṭa, (Viv. I. Th. I, p. 283) the object of the Wrong Cognition is the external *this*-element of the Shell.

The *Yogasūṭra* accepts the Naiyāyika view of Wrong Cognition. It defines *Viparyaya*, or Wrong Cognition, as 'a notion which abides in a form which is not that of its object' (I—8); and the *Bhojavriṭṭi* adds—'it is a notion of something in respect of which it really is not,' '*aṭaṭhābhūṭērṭhē ṭaṭha uṭpaḍyamānam,'*—which comes to the same thing as the '*aṭasmin ṭaḍiṭi,*' of the *Nyāyavārṭika.*

It has been held that the wrong cognition is sublated by a subsequent right cognition. What is the nature of this 'sublation'? What is meant by a cognition being 'sublated'? This means that the cognition is bereft or deprived of its objective (Nyā. Mañj., p. 186); that is to say, the object apprehended by the cognition becomes deprived of its *apprehendedness;* that is, it is made known that the *apprehendedness* was unreal. The sublating cognition appears in the form—'What I had, on the former occasion, apprehended as silver was not silver, but something else,'—which means that the *apprehendedness* of the silver was not true. Another explanation of 'sublation' suggested is the being deprived of its fruit; the fruit of the cognition of a thing consists in its being acquired or discarded; in the case of the wrong cognition of silver, when the resultant acquiring comes, it is found not to pertain to silver; so that the cognition of silver becomes deprived of its fruit.

As Dream is only one of the many kinds of Wrong Cognition, this is the best place for enquiring into the account given by Indian philosophers of the exact character of Dreams.

The Vēḍānṭa view of Dreams, and of their difference from ordinary Wrong Cognition, is thus briefly explained by Viḍyāraṇya (Viv. Pra. Saṅ., I. Th. I, p. 283 &c.):

'In the waking state the contact of the sense-organ with the external object produces a modification of the internal organ which has for its object the external *this*-element of the shell and the like; for the internal organ has no independent energy outside the body. In dreams on the other hand, the internal organ, which, within the body, is independent—may function on its own account and is not, therefore, dependent on contact with external objects. The third cause—*viz.*, the modification of the internal organ—is thus present in dreams no less than in the waking state. The substrate also is in both cases the same;—*viz.* Consciousness circumscribed by the modification of the internal organ. The difference however is that in the case of the ordinary waking Wrong Cognition, the shell and the *this*-aspect are what bring about the contact of the sense organ.... The two cases therefore stand as follows: In the waking state, that Nescience—which has for its substrate Consciousness, as manifested by that modification of the internal organ which is due to the contact of the sense-organ and object, and as defined by the *this*-element of the shell,—illusorily projects itself in the form of silver; analogously, in the state of dream, there is concerned that Nescience, which has for its substrate Consciousness as defined or circumscribed by a certain modification of the internal organ—which modification originates within the body (independently of external objects) and is influenced by the defect of drowsiness and the like;—this Nescience, being at the same time assisted by the mental impressions left behind by previous perceptions—which, at the time are revived by the Unseen Principle,—illusorily projects itself in the form of the world of things that are seen by the dreaming person.

The Mīmāmsaka view of Dreams has already been explained above.

The Vaishēṣika Prashastapāḍa-Bhāṣya provides the following account of Dreams:

The mind having retired within the trans-organic regions of the Soul, and thereby the functioning of the sense-organs having ceased, by reason of drowsiness, which is brought about by the contact of the Soul with the Mind, and by reason also of the impressions of previous perceptions, there appear cognitions in the form of Perception; and it is this pseudo-perception during sleep that is known as 'Dream.'

Dreams have been divided into three classes: (1) those caused by the force of the extra-vivid impressions left by previous perceptions; when, for instance, a banker dreams of his money; (2) those due to the derangement of the bodily humours; as, when, on account of the wind-humour being excessive, one dreams of flying in the sky; (3) those due entirely to the Unseen Agency of the person's merit and demerit; *e.g.* when one dreams of riding an elephant and such other things as are regarded to be indicative of good or evil to come.

CHAPTER IV

Doubt

We have dealt with the first two kinds of Direct Apprehension—Right Cognition and Wrong Cognition. We now take up the third kind, Doubtful Cognition. Doubt, as forming the basis of all Discussion, is the third item in Gauṭama's scheme; and as such its treatment should, in the ordinary course, have come after the Objects of Cognition had been dealt with but we may deal with it here; as after all, Doubt is only a form of Cognition.

The Nyāya-Sūtra (1-1-23) defines *Doubt* as 'that wavering judgment in which definite cognition of the specific character of any one object is wanting, and which arises—(a) either from the cognition of properties common to the objects concerned; (b) or from the cognition of properties that serve to distinguish an object from diverse homogeneous and heterogeneous objects; and (c) from the presence of contradictory opinions; and the appearing of such wavering judgments is due to the uncertainty attaching to perceptions and non-perceptions.'

The Bhāṣya supplies the following explanation: (a) The first kind of Doubt is that which arises from the cognition of properties common to two things *e.g.* when, in a certain object seen by us we are cognisant of only such properties as are common to two things—as for instance, of the quality of *tallness* only—and we do not perceive any qualities that would help us in determining if what we see is a man or a pillar,—there arises in our mind the wavering judgment—'May this be a man or a pillar?' (b) The second kind is that which arises from the cognition of properties that serve to distinguish an object from diverse (homogeneous and heterogeneous) objects, *e.g.* in the case of many objects we find that their special properties distinguish them from homogeneous as well as heterogeneous objects; for instance, the earth is distinguished by the property of odorousness; and this distinguishes it from Water, Fire, &c., which are homogeneous to it, as being 'Substance,'—as also from such heterogeneous things as *Action* and the rest; hence even when we perceive only odorousness in a clod of earth,—and do not perceive those other wider qualities which mark it as *Substance*—we are in doubt as to whether it is a *Substance* or an *Action.* (c) The third kind of Doubt arises from the presence of contradiction; *i.e.* from the presence of opposite statements about an object; *e.g.* one philosophy asserts that Soul exists, while another holds that there is no such thing as Soul; so long as we do not find any reasons helping us to determine in favour of either of the two alternatives, we have a doubt on the point. Doubt is due to the uncertainty of perception, as when we know that there has been perception of water where water was actually present; as in the lake; and there has been perception of water also where water was not present; as in the mirage; so, whenever we have perception of water, there is always an uncertainty as to whether there is water or something else appearing like water. Doubt is also due to the uncertainty attaching to non-perception: Seeing that the water in the roots and branches of trees, though present, is not perceived,—even when we do not see water in a certain place, we are in doubt as to whether water is actually absent or not. (Vā. Bhā., pp. 34-35).

The above statement of the Bhāṣya has been taken to mean that there are five kinds of doubt. For instance, the Nyāyamañjarī (p. 562) says इति पञ्चविध: प्रपञ्चितो मुनिना दर्शित एषसंशय: But the Vārṭika and the Ṭāṭparya both hold to the three-fold division of Doubt, as detailed under (a), (b) and (c), the first three explained above; and the subsequent phrase is regarded as affording an explanation applicable to all Doubts; and the Ṭāṭparya says that the five-fold division should be discarded. Nor is there anything definite in the Bhāṣya itself to justify the five-fold division; though such a division appears to be implied by the way in which the Bhāṣya has explained the Sūṭra.

The above Explanation of Doubt has been accepted by the modern Naiyāyika. Says the *Tarkabhāṣā* (pp. 63-64, Indian Thought II, pp. 103-104).

'When with reference to one and the same object there arise ideas of two mutually contradictory things, it is what is called 'Doubt'. It is of three kinds: (1) Arising from the non-perception of the difference between two things, and the perception of only their similarities; (2) Arising from difference of opinions; and (3) Arising from the perception of a property that is peculiar to the thing concerned. (1) As an instance of Doubt arising from the perception of similarities, and non-perception of differences, we have the doubt as to the object seen being 'a man or a post;' in this case, with reference to the object seen, when the observer fails to perceive either the presence of crooked crevices, which would lead to its being definitely recognised as the post, or the presence of hands, head and other limbs, which would indicate it definitely to be a *man*,—and he perceives only the tallness and such other properties common to the man and the post—he has the doubt in the form 'is this a post or a man?' (2) The second kind of doubt is that which is due to there being differences of opinion, and the distinctive features not being perceived; *e.g.* the doubt as to words being eternal or non-eternal. Some philosophers hold that words are eternal, while others regard it as non-eternal; and the impartial man who becomes apprised of this difference of opinion, and does not himself notice any such features in Words as would point definitely one way or the other, has the doubt—'is Word eternal or non-eternal?' (3) The third form of Doubt is that which is due to the perception of a property that is peculiar to the thing in question only; *e.g.* when one perceives the presence of odour in a clod of earth,—which is a property peculiar to earth only, which does not indicate either its eternality nor non-eternality—and he does not notice any other property favouring either eternality or non-eternality, there arises in his mind a doubt as to earth being eternal or non-eternal; the doubt appearing in the form—'Is the Earth eternal, because possessed of the quality of odour which is not present in many non-eternal substances, like a piece of ice and such other aqueous products? Or is it non-eternal, because possessed of the quality of odour which is present in many non-eternal substances, like the jar and other things?'

The Nyāyamañjarī, p. 556, notices another explanation of the Sūṭra by which Doubt is defined simply as 'wavering judgment,' or as 'wavering judgment due to the perception of similarities;' and the rest of Sūṭra is regarded as purely explanatory.

The Vaishēṣikas divide Cognition into two classes—Knowledge and Ignorance. Under Ignorance they have, (1) Doubt, (in the form 'is the thing I perceive this or that?'), (2) Wrong Cognition (when a thing is known as what it is not), (3) Uncertain Cognition (in the form 'what may this be?'), and (4) Dream. Under *Knowledge* they have Perception, Inference, Remembrance and Intuition. (Prashasṭapāḍa, under 'Buḍḍhi.')

The Mīmāmsaka view is as follows:

As regard Doubtful Cognitions—*e.g.* 'is this a pillar or a man?'—what is actually perceived is some object endowed with the quality of *tallness*; and this is quite valid so far. This perception of tallness then brings to the mind of the observer a number of *tall* things, the pillar, the man, the tree, and so forth; then it is that there comes the doubt as to whether the object before the eyes is this or that particular *tall thing.* Thus in all doubtful cognitions there are two remembrances involved; there is not only one act of apprehension.' (*Prābhā. Mīmā.*, p. 32.)

CHAPTER V

Remembrance

We have dealt with Right Cognition, Wrong Cognition and Doubtful Cognition, which are the three kinds of Direct Apprehension or *Anubhava,* the first kind of Cognition. We now proceed to deal with the second kind of Cognition, *Smaraṇa,* as distinguished from Direct Apprehension.

In the course of argument in favour of the view that all cognitions belong to the Soul, the Bhāṣya (pp. 177-78) says—

'Remembrance is the cognizance by a man of what has been cognised before by the same man; the cognitive agent being the same in both cases; which shows that one to whom cognitions—Direct Apprehension as well as Remembrance—belong must be a lasting entity, and not anything ephemeral or transient. The entity to whom Remembrance belongs must be the same to whom the original cognition of the thing belonged.'

The earliest definition of Remembrance that we have found is that supplied by Patañjali in his Yogasūṭra, where under Sūṭra 1-11, we find Remembrance defined as 'the non-relinquishment of an object that has been cognised';— 'non-relinquishment' being explained as 'not allowing to escape from our mind an object which has once been cognised through the proper means of knowledge' (Bhojavṛiṭṭi); and the psychology of Remembrance is thus explained by Vyāsa in his Bhāṣya on this Sūṭra—'The cognition, coloured by the cognised object, and as such manifesting or illuminating the forms of both (the object as well as the cognition), produces an impression of the same character; and this impression, being of the same form as its cause, brings about a re-collection, a re-cognizance, which also partakes of the same character.' On this the Vāchaspaṭya notes—'The definition of Remembrance thus comes to be this, that, it is that function (of the Mind) which has for its object something that has already been the object of a previous function; and this is the *non-relinquishment* of the object spoken of in the Sūṭra.' The *Bhāṣya* proceeds 'This Remembrance is two-fold: one in which the object remembered is purely imaginary, and the other in which the object is not imaginary; the former we have during dreams, and the latter in the ordinary waking state.'

In the *Tarkabhāṣā* (p. 61) we read that Remembrance is of two kinds, Right and Wrong; according as it is, or it is not, in consonance with the real character of the object remembered; both those kinds appear during the waking state; and during Dreams the element of Remembrance present is always of the wrong kind, not necessarily because the object dreamt of does not exist in reality (as very often the things we dream of really exist), but because, not being actually in contact with any means of direct cognition, the obejct, during a dream, should be known as 'that,' something not before the eyes; while, as a matter of fact, it is known as 'this;' and it is in this that the *wrongness* of the Remembrance lies.

Gauṭama's Sūṭra 3.2. 43-44, afford material for an interesting study of the psychology of Memory and of the association of ideas in general. In this Suṭra Gauṭama enumerates the various causes that lead to the remembrance of things, and form the basis of Memory:

(1) Attentiveness: fixing the mind on what is to be remembered; (2) Association: fixing some connection among diverse things, whereby they may help the remembrance of one another; or fixing of them in the mind; (3) the Faculty of Memory acquired by frequent repetition; (4) Correlated Indicatives: things related either by contact, as smoke indicates fire, or by inherence in a common substratum; as the hands or the feet; or by contradiction; as what exists brings to mind what does not exist; (5) Characteristic features, *e.g.*: the features of the animal brings to mind the entire species to which the animal belongs; (6) Similarity: *e.g.* the picture reminds us of the original; (7) Possession: as where the possessor of a horse reminds us of the horse; (8) Supporting: as when the master reminds us of the servant; (9) Being supported: as when the servant reminds us of the master; (10) Relationship: as when the pupil reminds us of the teacher; (11) Sequence: when in the details of a performance, the performance of one item reminds us of the item that follows it; (12) Separation: when two separated lovers are reminded of each other; (13) Identity of work or function: when one bricklayer reminds us of another of the same trade; (14) Enmity: when of two competitors the sight of one brings the other to the mind; (15) Excess: reminds us of what brings about the excess; (16) Attainment: one often remembers what he has to acquire; (17) Concealment: when the case of a cocoon reminds us of the insect that has gone out of it; (18) Pleasure and Pain: bring to mind what causes them; (19) Desire and Aversion remind us of their objects; (20) Fear: brings to mind the source of fear; (21) Longing: is the cause of the remembrance of what is desired; (22) Action or Profession: as the sight of the chariot reminds us of the carpenter who made it; (23) Love: reminds us of the beloved; (24) Merit: brings the memory of past lives, and also that keenness of memory which helps in study, &c.; (25) Demerit: puts us in mind of unthought of sources of pain and suffering. This list is not meant to be exhaustive; it is purely suggestive. In short,

what brings about Remembrance is that faculty which is brought into existence by cognitions; and Remembrance is not the direct result of cognitions.

The *Tarkabhāṣā* also says that the Faculty of *Bhāvanā* is produced by Direct Apprehension, and, in its turn, produces Remembrance; but only when it is energised by the presence of accessory aids in the shape of the Perception of similar things Unseen Agency, Constant Thought (and the rest, enumerated in the aforesaid Sūṭra).

According to Vaishēṣika-Sūṭra 9-2-6: Remembrance is brought about by the contact of the Soul with the Mind and by impression. On which the Upaskāra remarks: 'In remembrance the particular Mind-Soul contact is the non-material (indirect) cause; the impression is the efficient (direct) cause; and the Soul the material cause;' and the Prashasṭapāḍa-Bhāṣya: "Remembrance of past things is brought about by a particular kind of Mind-Soul contact due to the perception of indicative signs, or to desire, or to subsidiary remembrance; also by impression or faculty caused by impressive cognitions, or by repeated cognitions or by attentive cognitions; and this Remembrance appears with regard to things perceived, or heard of, or otherwise directly apprehended."

The Mīmāmsakas, agreeing with the above view, have held that Remembrance is produced only by the impressions left by a previous cognition. (Prābhā. Mīmā., p. 19.)

'The modern Naiyāyika also lays stress upon the *only*; as they hold that without this qualification, the definition would apply to Recognition, which also is produced by impressions left by previous cognitions. The older Naiyāyikas do not insists on this qualification; for they hold that Recognition is not brought about *by impression*, but by the *remembrance* of the character of the thing perceived. The moderns regard Recognition as brought about by the eye that perceives the thing, as aided by the impression left of its previous cognition.

The Māhḍhvas hold that Remembrance is brought about directly by the *Mind,* and not by impressions; and the Impression or Faculty is nothing apart from the contact of the Mind with the object.

The very fact of Remembrance forming a class apart from Direct Apprehension or *Anubhava* (of which latter Right Cognition is a sub-class) shows that the former is not Right Cognition or *Pramā.* Says the *Prābhākara:*

'Remembrance is not valid, inasmuch as it stands in need of a previous cognition, being, as it is, a cognition produced only by the impressions left by a previous cognition.'

That is to say, Remembrance cannot be ragarded as valid, because it bears upon its object, not *directly,* but only indirectly, through the agency of previous cognitions; (Prābhā. Mīmā., pp. 19-20) and Valid Cognition is always *direct.*

The Vaishēṣikas make Remembrance as valid as Perception and Inference; distinguishing it entirely from Ignorance of all kinds.

The Vedantic idea of Remembrance is thus put forth in the *Vivaraṇaprамēyasaṅgraha* (Text, p. 253).

'Remembrance is that conception which is dependent entirely on the energising of the impressions of the thing; and it never departs from the thing previously perceived; and it never affects any changes in the character of the thing. It is entirely independent of the man's will; often appearing in spite of his desire not to remember the thing, and not appearing when he seeks for it eagerly.'

So by this explanation there is nothing inherently invalid in Remembrance.

We have seen above that in defining Remembrance the Logician, ancient as well as modern, has drawn a distinction between Remembrance and Recognition:

The definition of Recognition given by Uḍayanāchārya in his Lakṣaṇāvalī is that it is that knowledge which is brought about by Impressions as aided by the sense-organs.

Before proceeding to explain in detail what Recognition is, we shall pause a little over the argument that the Bauḍḍha Idealist puts forward against the whole idea of Recognition. These arguments will also serve the purpose of showing the different views that have been held with regard to Recognition.

The Bauḍḍha insists on demolishing Recognition, as Recognition strikes at the root of the pet theory of the Bauḍḍha that everything has only a momentary existence. The Bauḍḍha position has been put forward in the *Nyāyamañjarī* (*Text,* pp. 448-50). It may be summed up as follows:

Recognition is said to be in the form 'this is that same jar;' now, does this involve one cognition, or a combination of two cognitions, or a direct apprehension and another a remembrance? If it is one, then it becomes necessary to examine the nature of the instrumentality that leads to it. The sense-organ can not bring about such a cognition; as no organ is in contact with the 'that'-element of the cognition; nor could it be due to impressions alone, as no impression can operate upon the 'this'-element; nor can the cognition be said to be brought about conjointly by the sense-organ and the impression; as in all cases, these two are found to operate separately, and never jointly; impression always leads to remembrance, and the sense-organ to direct apprehension; and there is no single effect that is ever found to have been brought about jointly by these; in no case is a mixed effect found to be produced by the joint action of the two different causes; for instance, no such thing as the *cloth-jar* is ever found to be produced by the joint action of yarn and clay. No sense-organ by itself is ever found capable of producing any such effect as appears in the Recognition. For these reasons Recognition must be regarded as involving two distinct cognitions—*a direct apprehension* so far as the cognition of 'this' is concerned, and a *remembrance* so far as concerns the cognition of ' that;' nor can there be any single cognition of any kind that partakes of the nature of both Direct Apprehension and Remembrance; for the simple reason that Remembrance pertains to what is remembered and Direct Apprehension to what it apprehended; in fact the cognitions of 'this' and 'that' involved in Recognition must be regarded to be as distinct as the Direct Apprehension of the jar and the remembrance of the cloth. Even if, for the sake of argument, we admit that Recognition represents a single cognition, we have to examine the character of the object of such a cognition. If the cognition apprehends a thing of the past, it is mere Remembrance; if it apprehends a thing of the future, it must be mere Imagination; if lastly, it apprehends only what exists at the present moment, then it does not prove that permanence of things which it is meant by the Logician to prove. Nor can it be held to apprehend a thing qualified by its previous cognition; as the previous cognition is not present at the time; and what is not present cannot serve as a qualification.

In answer to the above, the *Nyāyamañjarī.* (pp. 458-461), puts forward the *Nyāya* view of Recognition, which may be thus summed up:

As a matter of fact, there is a single idea or cognition involved in Recognition; and what brings about this cognition is the sense-organ assisted by impressions; it is true that sense-organs do not bring about such mixed cognitions;

but because such is generally the case, it is not necessary that it should be always so; it is perfectly legitimate for a cause to produce an effect different from its usual effect, when it has extraneous forces bearing upon it; and in the case in question, we have the force of impressions bearing upon the sense-organ, which, on that account, produces no effect in the shape of the mixed cognition involved in Recognition. As to the character of the object apprehended by Recognition, what is apprehended is an object that belongs to the present, but is qualified by the past time also; and when such is the actual fact it is idle to deny the possibility of such mixed character of the object. Nor need there be any incongruity in this; the past is cognised as 'past,' as 'that,' and the present is cognised as 'present,' as 'this;' and the idea of the object pervades over both; and is cognised as one and the same, related to both points of time. As to what is past, and hence not present at the time of the cognition, qualifying the object which is present, there is nothing incongruous in this either; *e.g.* when we are eating a number of fruits,—one hundred, for instance,—when we come to the hundredth fruit, we have the cognition of having eaten hundred fruits; this cognition being brought about, and qualified, by the fruits which had existed in the past, many seconds before the hundredth fruit is eaten and the number *hundred* recognised; and in reality, even though what is past is not present at the time, yet the relation that the object had with the past time is certainly present in the object; and qualification by this relation is all that is necessary for Recognition being coloured by the idea of the 'past.' Lastly, the Bauḍḍha has taken exception to the fact that Recognition, though partaking of the notion of what is past, is yet produced by the sense-object contact; but what incongruity is there in this? The object is there before the eyes; and there is thus present the sense-object contact which is the precursor of the Recognition; and when the object is seen, it is true that it is seen as qualified by the present time; but there is nothing to present its being, at the same time, known as qualified by the *past* time; this latter will be one among the many qualifications whose idea may quite reasonably come to the mind whenever the object is seen. Thus then, we come to the conclusion that Recognition apprehends objects that are present before the senses and which are qualified by the 'past' time; and they are brought about by the contact of the sense-organ with the object, and such other means of cognition;—or they may be held to have for their object, things qualified by the previous cognitions of themselves. Recognition thus is a form of qualified Perception.

The Vēḍānta view of Recognition is thus expounded in the *Vivaraṇapramēyasaṅgraha* (Trans. pp. 177-181, I. Th. I, pp. 405-9).

The Vedantins seeking to prove the permanence of Cognitions on the strength of Recognition, which according to these is an independent Means of true Knowledge, is met by the following arguments of the Bauḍḍha:

"Recognition cannot be regarded as immediate perceptive knowledge having for its object the relation of one thing to two points of time, a past one and the present one;—for perceptive knowledge apprehends present things only. It may be argued that Recognition must be of the nature of Perception, for it is originated by what is the cause of the valid cognition of a present thing—such cause being conjoined with the impression left by a previous perception (This view, it may be noted, is what has been put forward in the *Nyāyamañjarī*). But this does not satisfy us. As it does not meet the case of the Recognition of the Self which expresses itself in the form 'I *now* am the same person I was *then.*' For the Vedāntin's Self is eternal and self-illumined, and hence there can neither be an impression of it, nor can knowledge be originated in it. Nor again can Recognition be defined as neither more nor less than the cognition of a thing's essential nature; for such cognition, like the light of a lamp, illumines only what is present here and now, and hence does not imply reflexion on what is earlier and later—reflection of which kind is involved in Recognition. On the view of the Bauḍḍha Idealist the judgment 'I am the same person I formerly was' consists of two cognitions, each of which has its own specific character and is not a 'recognition.' As Recognition thus does not admit of a satisfactory definition you may not use it to prove the oneness and permanence of cognitions."

To the above the Vēḍantin offers the following reply:

Although Knowledge cannot indeed be originated in the pure Self, and there can be no impression of it, yet both these things are possible with regard to the Self qualified by the internal organ; and of this Self, therefore, there can be Recognition. This fact of the Self being the object of Recognition and at the same time the recognising subject, which means that one and the same thing is the object of an action and its agent, does not involve any incongruity in the case of the Self; for all philosophical schools are agreed that the Self is agent and object of action, in sor far as it is the object of certain inferential reasonings as to its difference from the body and similar things, and is of course the agent in all acts of cognising. And in the case of Recognition of the Self, the recognising agent is the Self in so far as qualified by the internal organ, and the object recognised is the Self in so far as qualified by earlier and later time; and it is the difference of conditioning adjuncts which renders it possible for the Self to be at the same time agent and object of action. It will be entirely unphilosophical to deny the actuality of Recognition. For Recognition, expressing itself in the form 'I now am the same person I formerly was,' is vouched for by our immediate consciousness; and as all men are agreed as to this, it cannot be treated as Error. The contention of the *Bauḍḍhas* that in the judgment 'I am that,' we have to do with two separate cognitions, each of which has its own specific character,—cannot be upheld; for were this so, we should have to conclude that also in the judgment 'cognition is momentary' (which is a proposition propounded by the Bauḍḍha), we have to do with two cognitions—*viz.*, (1) that 'Cognition *is*', and (2) that 'Cognition is momentary;' and in that case the theory of the momentariness of cognitions, which is the Bauḍḍha's great mainstay, could not be established. The upshot of all this is that Recognition may validly be conceived as Perceptive Cognition, with which there combines an impression left behind by a previous Perception; and on such Recognition also rests the incontestable consciousness of personal identity; for of, the Self, inasmuch as determined by self-consciousness, there may be a mental impression, and hence Remembrance and Recognition.

Prabhākara's view of Recognition does not differ from the above; but in his opinion, this permanent Self is established, not by the fact of its being the object of its own cognition, but by the fact of its being the substrate of the recognitive cognitions of other things. The consideration of Prabhākara's views of Self we must leave for a future occasion; but it is interesting to note in the present connexion the explanation that Prabhākara has provided of the view of the Self being both the object and agent of the act of cognition. It is true, says the Prābhākara, that the Self is cognised by the same means of valid cognition as the objects themselves; but even so the Self is not the *objective* but the *subjective* agent of the operation of cognition; just as even though the person who walks has the operation of walking bearing upon himself he is regarded only as the nominative agent of the walking, and not as its object; specially as a true object is that upon which bears the operation of something other than itself; and this is not the case with the Self, upon which its own action of cognition bears. (Prābhākara Mīmāmsā, p. 78).

CHAPTER VI

Cause

We have seen what Cognition is, and what are its principal sub-divisions. We revert now to the definition of Pramāṇa, the first topic of the Nyāyā-Sūṭra, for explaining the real character of which we found it necessary to explain Pramā or Right Cognition.

Pramāṇa has been defined as the 'instrument of right cognition;' we have explained what is 'right cognition.' We shall now proceed to consider what is meant of 'instrument,' '*karaṇa.*' 'Instrument is the name given'—says the *Tarkabhāṣa* (Trans., p. 42) 'to that particular cause which is the most effective in bringing about a certain result; *i.e.*, it is the most efficient cause; for instance in the action of *cutting,* though the operation of many things is necessary, such as the hand, the axe and so forth,—every one of which, on that account, is a 'cause' of the cutting,—it is the axe which is the *principal cause,* its operation bearing directly and immediately on the cutting; and on this account the axe is called the *karaṇa* or 'instrument' of the cutting.

Instrument thus being only a particular kind of cause, it becomes necessary for us to provide an account of 'Cause.' Though Gauṭama and Vāṭsyāyana have not dealt with this subject,—depending it would seem for an account of it, upon the sister system of the *Vaishēṣikas,*—yet, an account of the philosophy of Nyāya will remain incomplete in an important point, if we ignored the 'cause' altogether. Nor are we entirely at sea as to the Logician's standpoint in this connection. The later manuals provide us with an adequate account; and from these latter we learn the following details [*Tarkabhāṣā.* Trans., pp. 43-48].

That which must exist before the effect, and which is not taken up in the bringing about of something else, is to be regarded as the 'cause' of that effect; *e.g.* the yarn, the loom and such other things are the 'cause' of cloth; even though in some cases of the making of cloth, an ass may by chance come to the place, immediately before the making,—yet this mere *antecedence* does not make the ass a 'cause' of the cloth; because the previous presence of the ass is not *necessary* in the making of the cloth. Then again, even though the presence of the particular colour of the yarn is necessary, previous to the making of the cloth, yet that colour cannot be regarded as its 'cause,' as the colour is taken up in the bringing about of an entirely different effect, in the shape of the colour of the cloth woven out of those yarns. Thus then the cause of an effect may be defined as that *necessary antecedent which is not taken up in the bringing about of something else.* Similarly the effect of a cause is that *necessary consequent which is not brought about by any other cause.*

This Cause is of three kinds: (1) the *Samavāyi,* the material or constituent cause; (2) the *Asamanāyi,* the non-constituent cause; and (3) the *Nimiṭṭa,* the efficient cause or cause in general. The first of these is that which forms the material out of which, and inherent in which, the effect is produced; *e.g.* the yarns are the material cause of the cloth; as it is out of the yarns, never apart from these, that the cloth is produced; so that the relation between these is what has been called 'intimate' or 'inherent.' The non-material cause is that which is in close proximity to—*i.e.* inherent in—the material cause of an effect, and which has its causal efficiency towards a certain effect duly ascertained; *e.g.* the combination of the yarns is the non-material cause of the cloth; the combination, being a quality of the yarns, inheres in these yarns, which are the material cause of the cloth; and that the combination has its causal efficiency ascertained towards the cloth is shown by the fact that it is a *necessary antecedent* of the cloth, and 'is not taken up in the bringing about of any other effect;' these two being the only conditions necessary for causal efficiency. The Efficient Cause or Cause in General, is that which, while being neither the material, nor the non-material, cause, is yet 'a necessary antecedent not taken up in the bringing about of anything else;' *e.g.* the loom is such a cause of the cloth.

It is only things positive that have all three kinds of cause; of negative entities, there is only one kind of cause, the *Efficient;* and the reason for this lies in the fact that a negative entity cannot 'inhere' in, or have intimate relation with, anything.

From among these three kinds of causes, that which happens to be endowed with some sort of a special aptitude or efficiency is called the 'Instrument.'

As regards Right Cognition,—the Soul is its *material or constituent* cause; the contact of the Soul with the Mind is its *non-material* cause; and the thing known, and also the contact of the mind with the sense-organ, form its '*efficient*' cause.

According to the Nyāya the former two kinds of Cause are never regarded as 'instrument;' it is always the last kind that is so regarded; this is shown by the Bhāṣya declaring in regard to Perception, that if the cognition is the effect then the sense-organ is the 'instrument,' and if the acquiring or discarding of the perceived object are the effect, then the cognition is the 'instrument;' so that in neither case is either the Soul or the Soul's contact with mind spoken of as the 'instrument.'

With reference to the Pramāṇas, the Bhāṣya. (p. 10) raises a further question: 'Have the Pramāṇas their objectives in common? Or the scope of the Pramāṇas is restricted within mutually exclusive limits?' The answer given is that both of these are true: For instance, in the case of the Soul we find: (a) that it is by means of Word that we come to know that the Soul exist, (b) we find Inference operating upon it when it is asserted that 'the indicative marks of the Soul are desire, aversion &c.' (Sū.1.1. 10), which means that it is from the presence of these that the existence of the Soul is inferred; (c) and the Soul is also *perceived* by the peculiar contact of the Soul with the mind, this perception being the result of *yogic* trance, and as such possible only for the *yogin.* Thus it is found that the Soul forms an objective for all the four *pramāṇas.* Similarly in the case of fire, it is found that (a) when a trustworthy person tells us that there is fire at such and such a place, our cognition of fire is *verbal;* (b) drawing nearer to the place, if we happen to see smoke issuing from the place, we *infer* from this the presence of fire; (c) actually getting at the place, we directly *see* the fire. On the other hand, in the case of certain things we find that one thing is amenable to only one *particular pramāṇa; e.g.* that the Agnihotra should be performed by one who desires heaven we can know only from the *words* of the Veda; the ordinary man has no other means available for knowing this; similarly when we hear the sound of thundering, from this, we *infer* the source of the sound; and in regard to this we can have no Perception; nor any verbal cognition; lastly of our own hand we have only direct perceptive knowledge, and neither Inference nor Word is operative in this case.

Among the four kinds of Pramāṇas, Perception has been held to be the most predominant; for if a man seeks the knowledge of a certain thing, when he is told of it by a trustworthy person, and thereby has the verbal cognition of the thing, there is still a lurking desire in his mind to ratify this information by means of Inference through particular indicative features; and even after he has got at the inferential knowledge of the thing,—he is still desirous of *seeing* the thing with his own eyes; but when he has once *perceived* the thing directly, he does not seek for any other kind of knowledge of that thing. The examples cited above of the soul and fire, make this point clear. When the man has to know fire, if several *pramāṇas* come to bear upon it, as shown above, he has a commingling of the *pramāṇas*, in which case all longing for knowledge does not cease until the appearance of direct Perception; whereas if there is a single *pramāṇa* bearing upon the thing, there is no commingling, but separate functioning; and in this case also, it is Perception only that fully satisfies the inquisitive mind.

A further interesting question bearing upon *Pramāṇas* in general is discussed in Sūṭras 2.1.8 to 19. An objection is raised against the validity of Perception and the other *Pramāṇas*:

"Perception and the rest," it is argued, "can have no validity, as it cannot be shown whether they come before or after their object, or simultaneously with it. For instance, the cognition of odour is a Perception; if this existed before the odour, and the odour comes only afterwards, then the Perception is not produced by the contact of the sense-organ with the odour; and yet this is an essential condition in all Perception; according to Su. 1.1.4; *secondly* if the Perception comes *after* the odour; then before the appearance of Perception, what would be there to prove the existence of the odour? It is only by means of *Pramāṇa* that the existence of *pramēyas* can be proved; lastly, if the Perception is simultaneous with the odour, both coming into existence at the same time,—then, as a matter of fact, we find that many objects of cognition come into existence at a single time; for instance, when the jar is produced, there come into existence its odour, its colour, its size, and so forth,—all of which are objects of Perception; now all these cannot be the object of a single Perception; there are, in fact, as many perceptions as there are objects to be perceived; so that at the moment that odour and colour are produced, there will be produced, *ex-hypothesi,* also the perceptions of these; and thus we would have a simultaneity of cognitions; and this is against the Naiyāyika's tenet, as expressed in Sū. 1.1.16 and 3.2. 59. Thus then, all possible alternatives of the existence of Pramāṇa and its object having failed, the existence or validity of the Pramāṇas cannot be maintained." (Sū. 2.1. 8-11).

The answer to the above, as given by Vātṣyāyana (Bhā., p. 65, 1.12 *et. seq.),* is as follows:

As a matter of fact there can be no hard and fast rule as to the Pramāṇa coming before or after or simultaneously with its object. In some cases we find the means of cognition, the *pramāṇa,* appearing before the object; *e.g.* in the case of the light of the sun: the sun's light is the means by which we perceive things; so that when we perceive the jar that has just been made, we have the 'means'—in the shape of the sun's light—already in existence before the perceived object comes into existence;—on the other hand, in the case of lamp light we find that the lamp being lighted, we see things that have been in existence already; so that in this case, the 'means'—lamp-light—apears *after* the object; and lastly, in some cases both appear simultaneously; *e.g.* the inferential cognition of fire appears along with the cognition of smoke—where the latter cognition is the 'means' of the former. From these special cases we come to the conclusion that between the *object* and *what brings about its cognition,* that is the *Pramēya* and the *Pramāṇa,* there is no hard and fast rule as to the exact order in which the two appear.

Nor is there any such hard and fast rule as that what is once an 'instrument' is always an instrument; or that what is once an 'object' is always an object. For instance, the Self is an 'object' of cognition, as we are cognisant of it; but in regard to the cognition of other things, it is the 'cogniser;' similarly the axe is an *agent* when we say 'the axe stands here;' but it is an *object* when we say 'I see the axe;' and it is an *instrument* when we say 'I cut the tree with the axe;' it is the *dative* when we say 'I pour oil for the sake of the axe;' it is in the *ablative* when we say 'this piece of iron has fallen from the axe;' it is in the *locative* when we say 'the spot is on the axe.'

Under Sū. 2.1.17, the following further questions are raised: "How do you cognise the *Pramāṇas* themselves? By means of *Pramāṇa*? or without the instrumentality of *Pramāṇas*? If the latter, then, just as for the cognition of *Pramāṇas,* the instrumentality of *Pramāṇas* will not be necessary, so for the cognition of *Pramēyas* also; and there would thus be no need for postulating any *Pramāṇas* at all. If on the other hand, *Pramāṇas* are cognised by means of *Pramāṇas,* then, for the cognition of every single *Pramāṇa* you will have to postulate another *Pramāṇa;* for the cognition of this latter again, a third *Pramāṇa* would be needed and so and on, you would have to postulate *Pramāṇas ad infinitum.*

Then again, is one Perception cognised by means of Perception or by means of other *Pramāṇas?* If the latter, then, there would be more than four *Pramāṇas*? If the former, then is every Perception cognised by itself or by another Perception? If by another, then this another would be cognised by another, and so on and on, *ad infinitum.* If a

Perception is cognised by itself, then this involves the absurdity of the Perception operating upon itself. As a matter of fact, we do not find the sword-blade cutting itself. Hence the inevitable conclusion would appear to be that there is nothing by means of which *Pramāṇas* can be cognised.' *(Bhāṣya* and *Tāṭparya*, p. 255).

The answer to the above is supplied in Sū. 19.

In the case of lamp-light, which renders things visible, we find that the light itself is apprehended, made cognised, by a Perception other than that to which it itself gives rise. From this analogy we conclude that one Perception also is apprehended by means of another Perception. Among the several factors that enter into the perceptional process (1) the sense-organs are *inferred* as the essential instruments of the process; (2) the objects themselves are known by Perception; (3) the contact of the sense-organ with the perceived object is *inferred* from the fact that there is no Perception whenever there is anything intervening between the two and obstructing the contact; finally (4) the cognition produced by the sense-object contact (which cognition is what is the 'Perception' commonly so called) is perceived, like pleasure and pain, by means of the mind-soul contact, through its inherence in the Soul. When the Perception brings about the cognition of something else it is called '*pramāṇa;*' and when it is itself cognised, it is *pramēya;*' just as the lamp-light is called the *means* of seeing when it illumines objects; but it is known as the 'object perceived' when we look upon the light itself. Thus for the cognition of the *Pramāṇas* we do not require to postulate any additional *Pramāṇas*; nor need we hold the view that this cognition is not brought about by any instrumentality at all. (*Bhāṣya*, p. 71.) Nor is any Perception cognised by means of itself (*Tāṭparya*, p. 255). What is meant is that one Perception is cognised by means of another Perception. According to the *Naiyāyika* the mind is as much a sense-organ as any other;

and in the case of the perception of Perception, we have the same kind of sense-contact as we have in the case of the cognition of pleasure and pain; these latter, according to the *Naiyāyika* being perceived through their contact with the mind. Thus the cognition of Perception also, brought about by its contact with the mind-organ, becomes pure Perception. Then again, in the case of such conceptions as 'I am happy' we have the apprehension of 'I' by the apprehender himself;—and in the case of 'Mind' we find that we infer its existence by means of the mind itself, through the fact of the 'cognitions not being simultaneous.' Similarly there need be nothing incongruous in Perception being made known by itself.

It has been urged that if one Perception be held to be made known by another Perception, then for the knowledge, of this latter we would need another Perception; and so on *ad infinitum.* The answer to this is that we postulate things only in accordance with our requirements: we assume only such things as are absolutely necessary for the explaining of and the accounting for, well-known facts. Thus in the case in question, we find that when we perceive an object, we have one Perception; and this is invariably followed by a further conception 'I have perceived the object;' which means 'I know that the perceptional cognition of the object has appeared in my mind;' similarly when we infer something, we have the conception 'I know that an inferential cognition of the thing has appeared in my mind;' and so in every case, we find a cognition followed by a conception in the form of representative cognition or *anuvyavasāya;* now this representative cognition represents the former cognition as the object of a further cognition; and hence it becomes necessary for us to postulate a *Pramāṇa,* a means of knowing the former cognition. For the postulating of any further *Pramāṇas,* we have no such justification; as in our experience we never find any conception following after the aforesaid representative cognition; upon whose basis alone a further *Pramāṇa* could be postulated. Thus there can be no justification for the postulating of *Pramāṇas ad infinitum.*

Another answer to this objection is given by the *Tāṭparya Ṭīkā* (p. 256)–There are some *means of cognition* that produce other cognitions only when they have themselves been cognised: *e.g.* Smoke brings about the inference of fire only when it has itself been perceived; there are other means of cognition which, though producing other cognitions, themselves remain unknown: *e.g.* the Eye itself is not perceived at the time that it produces visual perception. This shows that it is not necessary for every *Pamāṇa* itself to be known in its turn by another *Pramāṇa;* hence also there can be no justification for postulating a *Pramāṇa* for the cognition of the aforesaid representative cognition.

Another interesting question arising from the above is– Are Perceptions cognised by Perceptions, Inferences by Inferences, Analogical cognitions by Analogical cognitions, and Verbal cognitions by Verbal cognitions? Or are all *Pramāṇas* cognised by means of Perception alone? or by Inference alone? or by Analogy alone? or by Words alone?

This question is not found raised either in the *Bhāṣya* or in the *Varṭika* or in the *Tāṭparya.* Not having raised the question, they do not provide any clear answer to it. All that the *Bhāṣya* says is–प्रत्याक्षादिभिरेव प्रत्यक्षादीनां यथादर्शन मुपलब्धिः 'It is by means of Perception and the rest that we have the apprehension of Perception and the rest,–just as we find in each individual case' (p. 71, line 10). The *Tāṭparya* also makes a similar assertion (pp. 255-56) प्रत्यक्षादिजातीयस्य प्रत्यक्षादिजातायेन ग्रहणमातिष्ठामहे 'What we hold is that what belongs to the category of Perception and the rest is apprehended by what belongs to the category of Perception and the rest.'

Both these assertions are vague; but from the mention of 'Perception *and the rest*' we can infer that cognitions are cognised not by means of any one *Pramāṇa,* but by various *Pramāṇas:* Sometimes a cognition may be direclty *perceived;* sometimes it may be *inferred* and so on. This is what is meant by what the Bhāṣya says (on p. 73) in regard to such assertions as 'my cognition is perceptional,' 'my cognition is inferential,' &c. &c. In most cases cognitions are cognised by means of Perception, - the Perception being obtained through the instrumentality of the Mind; as in the case of all cognitions the mind-soul contact is essential; and Mind being a sense-organ, the cognition brought about by its contact is 'perceptional.' This is the case in almost all cognitions by ourselves; but in some cases it happens, specially in regard to the cognition of other persons, that we can only *infer* the cognition; *e.g.* when we find a person fanning himself vigorously, from this action of his we infer that he has been feeling the heat; *i.e.* he has had the perceptional cognition of heat. Sometimes we find the man asserting 'I have seen an elephant,' in which case our cognition of this Perception of his is purely verbal. Lastly, when we find a man declaring, 'I am feeling the same pleasure that you are feeling,' our cognition of his perception of pleasure is analogical. There thus can be no hard and fast rule in regard to this matter. This is what the Bhāṣya (p.71) means by the qualifying word '*yaṭhāḍarshanan,*' 'just as we find in each individual case.' Roughly speaking, our own cognitions we cognise by means of Perception obtained through the contact of the Mind; while the cognitions of other people we cognise by means of Inference, Analogy and Word. And it is only in very rare cases, in cases of very vague perceptions that we may be led to *infer* our own cognitions.

This same question has been dealt with somewhat differently by Gaṅgēsha Upāḍhyāya in the *Ṭaṭṭvachinṭāmaṇi Prāmāṇayavāḍa,* p. 276:

It has been held that the validity of a cognition is cognised by another cognition. Now, is the validity of this latter cognition already known or not? If it is known, it must be so by a further cognition; and so on and on, there would be an endless series of cognitions. Another view held by some people is that the validity of the latter cognition is not already known from beforehand; but it is being known at the same time at which it apprehends the validity of the preceding cognition. This view is not right; as in that case, if the latter cognition were not to have its validity cognised by means of another cognition, then its validity would be self-apprehended;—a view which though held by the Prābhākara, is rejected by the Naiyāyika. The inevitable conclusion therefore is that when the validity of one cognition is apprehended by means of another cognition, the validity of this latter cognition is not apprehended at all. When such is the case with the latter cognition, the same may be said with regard to the first cognition also; that is to say, every cognition may be held to apprehend its object, without having its own validity apprehended; and there is no need for the ascertaining of this validity, when the definite cognition of the object is obtained without its ascertainment. It might be argued that the first cognition is often found to be invalid; so that unless its validity were ascertained, there would be no certainty in regard to the nature of the thing apprehended by it. But this same argument will also stand against the view that the validity of the second cognition need not be ascertained; as the uncertainty in regard to the validity of the second cognition will naturally reflect upon the validity of the first; and thus affect also the nature of the thing cognised.

The answer given to the above is that according to the Naiyāyika, it is not always absolutely necessary, for the obtaining of certainty with regard to an object, to ascertain the validity of the apprehending cognition. In the case of very clear cognitions, e.g. when we see a fruit in our hand—there is no doubt in our mind as to the validity of our cognition; and in such cases the definitely certain knowledge of the object is obtained by means of the first cognition itself, without any further thought over the validity or invalidity of that cognition; and when we act up to this knowledge, this activity of ours is found to be quite correct, and we actually find the fruit to be exactly what we had thought it to be on our first cognition of it. In some cases however,—when, *e.g.* we see an object, not seen before, for the first time in our life,—there is always a doubt in our mind as to whether or not our cognition apprehends the real thing as it actually exists; and in this case our resultant activity towards the object will naturally stand in need of that certainty which can be got at only by ascertaining the validity of the cognition that we have had; and it is only in such cases that it will be necessary to seek the aid of a further cognition to ascertain the validity of the former cognition; and so long as there is no doubt as to the validity of the second cognition, there is no need to seek for the ascertaining of its validity. When there is such a doubt, the assumption of a further validating cognition would be necessary; but only so long as there is any doubt. So there need be no assumptions *ad infinitum.*

CHAPTER VII

The Four Kinds of Right Cognition

'Perception, Inference, Analogy and Word are the Pramāṇas' says the Sūṭra (1-1-3).

Before dealing in detail with every one of these, we shall review in brief the explanations given of these, and supplement this with a review of the controversy over the precise number of Pramāṇas recognised.

Perception, says the Bhāṣya, consists in the functioning of each sense-organ upon a particular object, this 'functioning' being in the form either of *contact* or of *cognition*; when it is in the form of contact, then the result is in the form of right cognition; and when it is in the form of cognition, the result is in the form of the idea of the thing being discarded or chosen or treated with indifference. This is the earliest instance that we have of the double meaning that is always given to the word '*Pramāṇa.*' It is defined as 'the instrument of right cognition,' *i.e.*, the instrument that brings about the cognition of a certain thing; *e.g.* when the sense-contact of the thing brings about our perception of the jar. But the word is also used in the sense of 'form of cognition;' *e.g.*, in the case cited the perception itself is regarded as '*pramāṇa;*' and it fulfils the condition of being an 'instrument of cognition,' in virtue of its giving rise to the further cognition of the thing perceived being fit for being acquired or discarded or disregarded.

Here is what the *Vīrṭika* (p. 30) says on this double use of the word '*Pramāṇa*':

'In the case of all *pramāṇas*, when the word '*pramāṇa*' pertains to, or bears upon, itself, it denotes and accomplishes its own being; being, in this case, regarded as an abstract noun, it is synonymous with '*pramiṭi*' or cognition; when however it bears upon something else, the word '*pramāṇa*' denotes *instrumentality;* being explained, in this case, as *pramīyaṭē anēna,* that by means of which a thing is cognised; when the word is regarded as an abstract noun, and its result consists in the ideas that the observer has of discarding or accepting the thing cognised; it is only when an object has been duly cognised that we can have such ideas as that 'this thing should be discarded' and so forth. The view that the *contact* of sense-organ alone should be regarded as *Praṭyakṣa-pramāṇa* is rejected on the ground that, inasmuch as both, Contact and Cognition, are productive of definitive cognition, there is no reason why only one of these should be regarded as '*praṭyakṣa-pramāṇa.*'

Inference, says the *Bhāṣya,* is that after-cognition of a thing which is obtained though the agency of an indicative feature which is duly recognised, and which belongs to that particular thing.

Analogy as a *pramāṇa* consists in the cognition of approximation—*i.e.,* of the presence of common properties—says the *Bhāṣya.* The *Vārṭika* offers the following explanation: What happens in the case of all analogical cognitions is that the observer, who has seen the cow and is cognisant of its similarity to the unknown animal, happening to see that other animal, recalls to his mind the idea that had been afforded to him by means of words indicating the fact of the two animals being similar; and thereby coming to perceive directly the similarity in the animal before his eyes, he arrives at the cognition 'the name that I had heard mentioned belongs to this animal,' wherein he has the cognition of the connection of the thing with its name.

'Word is that by which objects are signified or denoted or made known'—*Bhāṣya*. That is, '*shabḍa*, as a *pramāṇa*, consists in the cognition of the denotation of words'—*Vārṭika*. The *Tāṭparya* affords the following explanation: 'When a sentence is uttered, there arises a cognition of things denoted by the words composing the sentence; and it is this cognition that constitutes '*shabḍa*' or 'word' as the fourth *Pramāṇa;* when this cognition is the *pramāṇa*, the 'means,' then the result consists in the knowledge of the meaning of the whole sentence; and when the cognition of the meaning of the entire sentence is the *pramāṇa*, then the result is in the form of the thing being known as to be discarded and so forth.

The Suṭra and the Bhāṣya have both enumerated the *pramāṇas* in a definite order; and various explanations have been given for this. Some people have offered the following explanation.

Perception has been mentioned first, as the most important of the four; after this comes Inference as it is always preceded by and based upon Perception; after Inference comes Analogy, as it is similar to Inference, both depending upon the remembrance of past cognitions; and Word comes last, because its scope is the vastest of all.

Some people have held that—there is no ulterior motive underlying the adoption of the particular order. When the author had to mention four things, he must have adopted some order; and he chose one at random, without regard to any special circumstances.

The explanation as suggested by the *Vārṭika* is somewhat different: Perception comes first, because it is the most important of all, supplying the foundation for all the other pramāṇas. Inference depends upon premisses which are afforded by Perception; Analogy also depends on the perception of common properties; and Word depends upon the perception—hearing—of the word—sound. Perception has also been regarded as the most important because of the fact that when a thing has been apprehended by Perception,—*i.e.*, has been directly perceived,—there is no further desire on the part of the observer to have any other cognition of it; it is not so in the case of other *pramāṇas.* When we are told that a certain thing that we want is to be found in a certain place, we are not satisfied with this verbal cognition; we go to the place, and are satisfied only when we have seen the thing there; after which there is no further search. Similarly when in search of fire a man sees smoke issuing from a certain spot, he infers the presence of fire; but is not satisfied until he has gone to the place and actually found and seen the fire.

The above explanation does not touch the precedence as among Inference, Analogy and Word. The real explanation appears to lie in the difference in the number of persons accepting the independent validity of the several Pramāṇas.

Perception is recognised by all men—the philosopher as well as the fool; Inference is recognised by the next largest number of persons—all philosophers accept it; Analogy comes next, as among philosophers there are many—*e.g.*, the Vaishēṣika and the Bauḍḍha and the Jaina—who do not accept it as a distinct Pramāṇa; and Word comes last, as this is not accepted, not only by the Bauḍḍha and the Vaishēṣika, but also by a party of Naiyāyikas also (says the *Nyāyakosha*); in regard to the exact nature of the validity attaching to verbal cognitions, there is a great difference of opinion among those who accept it as Pramāṇa; for instance, among the Naiyāyikas and the Mīmāmsakas.

The diversity in the classification of Pramāṇas accepted by the various philosophers is of two kinds. There is the diversity between the Materialist-Atheist and the Logician; the latter admitting four pramaṇas, while the Materialist admits only Perception, and discards Inference and the rest as not necessarily leading to any right knowledge. On the other hand, there is the diversity between the Logician and the Vēḍānṭin; the Vēḍānṭin admits Presumption as a right pramāna in addition to Perception, Inference, Analogy and Word admitted by the Logician; and the Vēḍānṭin admits this additional pramaṇa on the ground that the knowledge that it brings about is of a character entirely distinct from that obtained by the other four means; the Logician however does not admit Presumption; not indeed because Presumption does not lead to right knowledge; but because the right knowledge got by its means does not essentially differ from that got by means of Inference; so that as a means of knowledge, Presumption is only a form of Inference, and as such, not to be regarded as a distinct pramāṇa. Most of the diversity of opinion on this point is of this latter immaterial kind; we shall see this as we proceed. The *Nyāya-bhāṣya* distinctly declares (p. 101, under Sūṭra 2-2-2) that 'These (Tradition, Presumption, etc.), are certainly Pramāṇa; what we mean is that these are not distinct from the other *Pramāṇas.*' In fact under sūṭra 2-2-3—6, we have a vigorous defence of Arṭhāpaṭṭi against *apramāṇya* and similarly of Negation under sūṭra 2-2-7—12.

We shall first take up those philosophers the number of whose pramāṇas is less than four, the number admitted by the Logician.

First of all comes the *Chārvāka,* the Materialist-Atheist; who is said to admit the validity of Perception only. It is interesting to note the arguments with which the Materialist rejects the validity of inferential cognition; the argument is logical and very subtle and aims at proving the impossibility of any cognition that could be expressed by a universal proposition.

"Those who maintain the authority of Inference," says the Chārvāka, "accept the middle term as the cause of knowledge, which middle term must be found in the Minor, and be itself invariably connected with the Major Term. Now, this invariable connection must be a relation destitute of any (vitiating) condition, accepted or disputed; and this connection does not possess its power of causing inference by virtue of its *existence,* as the Eye, etc. are the cause of perception; but by virtue of its being *known.* What then is the means of this connection being known? We will first show that it is not Perception. Perception is held to be of two kinds, external and internal; that is as produced by the external senses, or by the inner-sense, mind. The former is not the required means, for although it is possible that the actual contact of the senses and the object will produce the knowledge of the particular object thus brought in contact, yet as there can never be such contact in the case of the past or the future, the universal proposition which has to embrace the invariable connection of the middle and major terms in every case, becomes impossible to be known.

"Nor is the internal perception the means; since you cannot establish that the mind has any power to act independently towards an external object; since all allow that it is dependent on the external senses....

"Nor can Inference be the means of the knowledge of the universal proposition; since in the case of this inference, we should also require another inference, to establish it and so on; and hence would arise the fallacy of an *ad infinitum* retrogression.

"Nor can Testimony be the means thereof. Since we may either allege in reply that it is included in Inference, in accordance with the Vaishēṣika doctrine of Kaṇāḍa; or else we may hold that this fresh proof of Testimony is unable to leap over the old barrier that stopped the progress of Inference; since it depends itself on the recognition of a sign, in the form of the language used in the child's presence by the old man; and moreover there is no reason for our believing another's word that smoke and fire are invariably connected.... And again, if Testimony were to be accepted as the only means of the knowledge of the universal proposition, then, in the case of man, to whom the fact of the invariable connection between the middle and major terms had not been pointed out by another person, there could be no inference of one thing on seeing another thing. Hence on your own showing the whole topic of inference for one's own benefit (where there is no assertion of propositions by another person) would have to end in mere idle words.

"Then again, Comparison (Analogy), etc., must be utterly rejected as the means of the knowledge of the universal proposition; since it is impossible that they can produce the knowledge of the unconditioned connection—*i.e.*, the universal proposition; the end is to produce the knowledge of quite another connection—*viz.*, the relation of a name to something named.

"Again, this same absence of condition, which has been given as the definition of an invariable connection, can itself never be known; since it is impossible to establish that conditions must be objects of perception; and therefore although the absence of perceptible things may be itself perceptible, the absence of non-perceptible things must be itself non-perceptible; and thus since here too we must have recourse to inference, etc., we cannot leap over the obstacle which has already been planted to bar these . . . .

"Since the knowledge of the condition must precede the knowledge of the condition's absence, it is only when there is the knowledge of the condition, that the knowledge of the universality of the proposition is possible; *i.e.,* a knowledge in the form of such a connection between the middle term and major term as is distinguished by the absence of any such condition; and on the other hand, the knowledge of the condition depends upon the knowledge of the invariable connection ['condition' having been defined as 'that which is equipollent in extension with, *i.e.* constantly accompanies, the major term, though not constantly accompanying the middle']. Thus we fasten on our opponents as with adamantine glue the thunderbolt-like fallacy of reasoning in a circle. Hence by the impossibility of knowing the universality of a proposition it becomes impossible to establish Inference, &c. The step which the mind takes from the knowledge of smoke to the knowledge of fire can be accounted for by its being based on a former perception, or by its being an error; and that in some cases this step is justified by the result, is accidental; just like the coincidence of effects observed in the employment of gems, charms, drugs, &c."

(*Sarvaḍarshanasaṅgraha,* Cowell and Gough, Ch. I.).

Another reason put forward against the validity of Inference is that no reliance can be placed on the universal proposition—'All men are mortal' for instance; it is true that the man making the assertion has found all men to be mortal; but it is just possible that in the future an immortal human being might turn up. This likelihood of contravention is inseparable from all universal propositions; and again when an inference has been presented to us, we cannot accept it as true; as it is just possible that the next moment an inference to the contrary may be presented to us by a man who has better opportunities of observation and a keener intellect than the former man. And so on and on; no implicit faith can be reposed on any Inference; which therefore cannot be regarded as authoritative.

We shall see what answer the Logician has to give to this, when we come to deal with *Inference* in detail.

The above account of Chārvāka's creed we have learnt from the *Sarvaḍarshanasaṅgraha.* But the *Nyāyamañjarī* declares on p. 36 that the "well-trained Chārvāka holds that the exact number of *pramāṇas* cannot be determined;" and again on p. 64,—

"The astute Chārvāka, having declared his intention, in his first *Sūṭra,* as 'I am going to explain truth,' has, in his work, 'explained the truth' by asserting that it is absolutely impossible to determine either the exact number or the exact character of Pramāṇas and Pramēyas, and in support of this he proceeds to cite instances of many cognitions that cannot be included in Perception, Inference, &c."

From these quotations it would appear that the author of the *Mañjārī* had access to the original *Sūṭras* of Chārvāka. And this shows that Chārvāka, does not hold the view that Perception is the only Pramāṇa,—as declared in the *Sarvaḍarshanasaṅgraha.* It appears that the author of this work had no access to any original work of the school, and, not without reason, came to the conclusion that as a rank materialist, a thoroughly worldly man, the Atheist could not deny the validity of Perception; and the author himself, being a skilled dialectician, thought, with justifiable pride perhaps, that every thinking man who accepted the validity of Inference, could not fail to be convinced of the existence of God; and thus the natural conclusion was that though the Atheist accepts the validity of Perception, he rejects that of Inference, and hence also of the other *pramāṇas.* But from the *Nyāyamañjarī* we learn the facts to be exactly the reverse. *Chārvāka* admits so many Pramāṇas that their enumeration is impossible. And as the *Mañjārī* actually quotes an original

Chārvāka *sūṭra,* we feel inclined to believe that its presentation of the system, obtained first-hand, is more reliable than that by the *Sarvaḍarshanasaṅgraha.*

Bauḍḍha View

From Diṅnāga's *Pramāṇasamuchchaya* and from Ḍharmakīrṭi's *Nyāyabinḍu* we learn that 'Valid Knowledge is of two kinds—Perception and Inference.' In Chapter IV of his *Pramāṇasamuchchaya* 'Diṅnāga rejects Comparison or Analogy as a separate source of knowledge; he says that when we recognise a thing through Perception of similar thing, we really perform an act of Perception. Hence comparison or recognition of similarity is not a separate source of knowledge, but is included in Perception. In Chapter V he rejects Credible Word as a separate source of knowledge. He asks 'What is the significance of a credible word? Does it mean that the person who spoke the word is credible, or the fact he averred is credible? If the person is credible, it is a mere Inference. On the other hand, if the fact is credible, it is a case of Perception. Hence the conclusion is that Credible Word is not a separate source of knowledge, but is included in Perception and Inference.

(*Medieval Logic*—Satish Chandra Vidyabhūsana, p. 88.)

We thus see that the Bauḍḍha philosopher does not reject the authority of Analogy and Word; but only objects to these being regarded as separate sources of knowledge.

The earliest Logician's answer to this we find in the *Nyaya-vārtīka* under Sūṭra 1-1-7. An we shall explain this under 'Analogy' and 'Word' later on.

Jaina View

As regards the Jaina view, we find the following in the *Nyāyāvaṭāra* the earliest Jaina work on Pure Logic:

"Valid Knowledge is divided into '*Pratyakṣa*' (Direct Knowledge) and '*Parokṣa,*' (Indirect Knowledge), including in the latter '*Anumāna*' (Inference) and 'Shabḍa' (Verbal testimony). This division contravenes the conclusion of Chārvāka that there is only one pramāṇa, *viz.*, *pratyakṣa*. Chārvāka's view is unreasonable; for *pratyakṣa* cannot be established as *pramāṇa* except through the medium of *parokṣa* or indirect knowledge. It also sets aside the view of the Bauḍḍhas, who divide *pramāṇa* into *pratyakṣa* and *Anumāna,* without any notice of *Shabḍa*" (p. 13 Trans).

The Nyāyāvaṭāra does not make any mention of either *Arṭhāpaṭṭi* or *Anupalabḍhi;* but from the above quotation it is clear that the Jainas do not accept any *pramāṇas* except the three therein described.

The *Bhāṣya* on the *Ṭaṭṭvārṭhāḍhigama Sūṭra,* another authoritative Jaina work however, under sūṭra 1.12 *et seq.*, speaks of *Anumāna* or Inference along with *Arṭhāpaṭṭi* and the rest; and with regard to these it says "Why are *Anumāna, Upamāna, Arṭhāpaṭṭi, Sambhava, and Abhāva,* which also are *pramāṇas,* not mentioned in the Sūṭra?" The answer to this is that all these are included under the category of '*parokṣa;*' then again, these five, Inference and the rest, may not be regarded as *pramāṇa* at all, inasmuch as they consist of wrong knowledge also.

Thus with regard to Inference, the Jaina position does not appear to be quite clear. The '*praṭyakṣa*' also of the *Ṭaṭṭvārṭhāḍhigama Sūṭra* is not the same as what other philosophers understand by the term. It is, according to the Bhāṣya on Sūṭra 1-12, 'beyond the reach of the senses; and the cognitions usually included under '*Praṭyaksa*' *e.g.*, the sensations of touch, colour, smell, sound, and taste—are classed (Bhāṣya on Sūṭra 1-14) under 'Parokṣa' or Indirect Knowledge. Under 'Indirect Knowledge' are also included Remembrance, Recognition, Ratiocination, Credible Word and Inference (as stated by a note on Verse 31 of the *Puruṣārṭhasiḍḍhyupāya);* all these, it appears, have been regarded as included under the *'māṭi'* or 'functionings of the Mind' of the *Ṭaṭṭvārṭhāḍhigama Sūṭra.*

The *Nyāyakosha* is not very accurate when it attributes only *two pramāṇas* to the 'Ārhaṭas.'

Vaishēṣika View

According to the *Vaishēṣikas,* there are four kinds of *Viḍyā,* Knowledge: Perception, Inference, Remembrance and Intuitional or Spiritual. That which is produced by sense-contact is Perception; that got at by means of an indicative mark, which is related to the object inferred and is never found apart from it, is Inference; the recalling of a previous cognition through certain causes is Remembrance; that which is entirely due to a supernatural faculty due to virtue and penance is called intuitional or spiritual cognition. Verbal cognition, according to the Vaishēṣikas, is only a form of Inference (*Prasthasṭapāḍa,* page 213); so also are Analogical Cognition (page 220), Presumptive Cognition (page 223), Probability (page 225), and Non-apprehension (page 225). It is not that these are not valid knowledge; they are as valid as Perception or Inference, but inasmuch as they can be reduced to the form of inference, there is no need for postulating them as distinct forms of valid knowledge.

With regard to Remembrance, the *Nyāyakanḍalī* (page 257) remarks that it is not *'Pramāṇa,'* as it apprehends past objects, and therefore depends upon a previous cognition, and is not independent, as pramāṇa should be.

But the *Bhāṣya* mentions Remembṛance along with the other three, and does not imply any such distinction as that while the other three are *pramāṇa,* Remembrance is not so. Nor is there any justification for the exclusion of Remembrance by the *Kanḍalī* itself; as the definition of

'*Viḍyā*' that it has provided (on page 172) is meant apparently to be a definition of '*Pramāṇa;*' this definition is— 'that well-difined cognition which is free from doubt, not liable to subsequent sublation;' and moreover on page 186, line 11, it calls all the three—Perception, Inference and Remembrance—'*laukika*' or human '*pramāṇa,*' as distinguished from the *spiritual cognition,* which is superhuman. So it appears it was only an afterthought which made the *Kandalīkārā* reject the *pramāṇaṭva* of Remembrance. Later *Vaishēṣika* writers have of course rejected its validity; but as time wore on and originality began to lose ground, the Nyāya and Vaishēṣika writers began to bring about a coalition between the two systems; so that in later literature, we find their angularities worn off, and the two philosophies mingled up almost beyond recognition, in the later manuals.

Sāṅkhya View

The Sāṅkhya view is thus put forth in the fourth Kārikā of Īshvarakṛīṣṇa—

'Perception, Inference and Valid Testimony are the three kinds of proofs necessary; these include all kinds of proofs.'

On this the *Ṭaṭṭvakaumuḍī* remarks—

"Proof is that by which right knowledge is determined, it is the means of correct cognition; correct cognition being a mental condition free from all that is doubtful, self-contradictory or unknown...... Proof is distinguished from all that leads to wrong notion; viz., doubt, misconception, memory and the like.'

These three, Perception, Inference and Valid Testimony, include all proofs. Analogy, according to the Sāṅkhyas, is included in Valid Testimony; so ṭhat Analogical cognition is only a form of Verbal Cognition. Presumption and Probability are included in Inference; and Non-apprehension in Perception. (*Ṭaṭṭvakaumuḍī,* on *Kārikā 5*).

So that according to the Sāṅkhyas also Analogy and the rest are *pramāṇa;* but do not differ from the three mentioned in the *Kārikā*; and Remembrance is not *pramāṇa.*

The *Yogasūṭra* also speaks of three forms of Right Knowledge: Perception, Inference and Valid Testimony, (Sūṭra 1-7). Neither the Sūṭra nor the Bhāṣya nor any of the more authoritative commentaries say anything as to the other pramāṇas, Analogy, Presumption and the rest.

Perception, according to the Yoga-Bhāṣya, is that function of the internal organ which has the external thing for its object, and which has its principal concern the ascertainment of a certain specific aspect of the object,—such functioning of the inner organ arising when it is affected by the external object through the pathway of the sense-organs;—Inference is that functioning of the inner organ which has for its object the relation that associates the object with all homogeneous objects and dissociates it from all heterogeneous ones: and this functioning is concerned chiefly with the ascertainment of the generic character of things; And lastly a certain object having been known by a trustworthy person, when that person expresses that cognition by words, for the purpose of conveying that knowledge to other persons, there comes about, by means of these Words, a functioning in the internal organ of the person addressed, which represents a form of knowledge that is called 'verbal.'

CHAPTER VIII

Perception

The general character of *Pramāṇa* or Instrument and Form of Right Cognition has been described. We have also seen that there are four such Instruments: Perception, Inference, Analogy and Word. We shall now take up each of these individually.

Perception has been defined by the *Sūṭra* and this definition has been accepted by the later writers as 'that cognition (a) which is produced by the contact of the object with the sense-organ, (b) which is not expressible by words, (c) which is not erroneous and (d) which is well-defined' (Sū. 1-1-4).

What are the 'sense-organs' and what the 'objects' we shall explain under the second category of Pramēya; the former have been described under Sū. 1-1-12 and the latter under Sū. 1-1-14.

In this definition we find four distinctive features laid down with regard to Perception: (A) it is produced by the sense-object contact, (B) it is not expressible by words, (C) it is not erroneous and (D) it is well-defined.

(A) The first part of the definition is that Perception is the cognition that is produced by the contact of the sense-organ with the object cognised. Against this the following objection is raised: "If such is the definition of Perception, then it is not right to hold, as the Logician does, that in all Perceptions the Soul is in contact with the mind, the mind with the sense-organ and the sense-organ with the cognised object; as the Sūṭra lays down only the contact of the sense-organ with the object as the necessary condition in Perception."

The answer to this objection is that the Sūṭra does not provide an exhaustive enumeration of all the factors that enter into the agency bringing about Perception; it does not mean that what is mentioned in the Sūṭra is the only cause of Perception; all that is meant is to indicate that factor which pertains to Perception exclusively, and which distinguishes it from all other forms of cognition; and it omits to mention the other factors—the contact of the mind with the soul and so on—not because these are not operative in Perception, but because they are common to Inference and other forms of cognition also. "Even so," the objector urges—"it was necessary to mention the contact of the mind with the sense-organ,—a factor which is peculiar to Perception and is not present in the case of other forms of cognition." As a matter of fact, the *Bhāṣya* replies, the contact of the mind with the sense-organ is not mentioned because when Perceptional cognition is distinguished from the other forms of cognition, that contact is as good a distinctive feature of its as the contact of the sense-organ with the object; consequently when one distinctive feature had been mentioned, there was no need for the mention of other similar features,—as the Sūṭra is not meant to be an exhaustive enumeration of all that distinguishes Perception from Inference and the rest. Another explanation suggested by the *Vārṭika* is that the *Sūṭra* mentions the sense—object contact only, because it is the peculiarity of sense-contact that distinguishes one perception from another perception; and it is in terms of the particular sense-contact, that each individual perception is spoken of; which is never in terms of the mind-organ contact. Whenever there is a perception, the *Vārṭika* explains, it is called either after the organ, or after the object; the perception of colour is called either 'visual perception' or 'colour-perception;' and no perception is ever called after the mind-contact: the perception of colour is never called 'mental perception.' Another explanation suggested by and preferred by the *Vārṭika* is that the mind-contact is not mentioned as the distinctive feature of Perception, as in regard to Perception that contact stands on the same footing as the Soul-contact; firstly because perceptions are never named after the Mind, nor after the Soul; and secondly because these two contacts—mind-contact and soul-contact—subsist in a substratum which is imperceptible by the senses; thirdly because neither of these two contacts belongs to the perceived object; and lastly because both belong to the mind.

In connection with this subject of *sense-organ contact* being the principal cause of Perception, the *Vārṭika* raises an interesting question:

"It is not right," the Opponent is represented as arguing, "to define Perception as produced by the *contact* of the sense-organ with the object; becasue as a matter of fact all the sense-organs operate upon objects without actually getting at, and being in touch with, them; so that no real contact is possible. For instance, according to some philosophers, both the Eye and the Ear are operative without getting at the objects; and in supports of this view, they put forward the following arguments: (a) It is a matter of common experience that we see, with our Eye, a thing which is lying at a place far off from ourselves; and certainly in this case it is not possible for the Eye to get at the thing seen; specially as the organ is only a material substance, and as such, incapable, by itself, to move up to a remote object; that which is called the 'Eye' is only the black material substance in the shape of the dark pupil, which is aided in its operation by another material substance, in the shape of light, outside itself, and further depends upon the *desire to see* on the part of the person to whose body the dark spot belongs, and also upon the past *Karman* of that person, conducive to the experiencing by him of the pleasure or pain due to that visual perception. That is to say, the Eye becomes the means of perceiving colour, because it is brought into existence by the past *Karman* that is conducive to the experiencing of colour as preceded by a desire for that experience. Similarly with the other sense-organs also. Thus then, the Eye-ball, which, by the above definition, is the visual organ, aided by another material substance in the shape of light, cannot possibly get at the object apprehended by its means. Hence we conclude that the Eye is operative without getting at the object, because it apprehends remote things. (b) Another reason for regarding the Eye as operative without getting at the object, lies in the fact that it apprehends things of larger and varying dimensions; if it were necessary for the Eye to get at the apprehended object, we could see only those things that are of the same size as the Eye; as only such things could be *got at* by the Eye, the Eye can never *get at* the entire elephant that is seen; and as a matter of fact we see such things of varying dimensions as the fly, the dog, the horse, the elephant, the sky, and the like. (c) A third reason for the same view lies in the fact that in the case of perception by the eye, there is always a mention of the particular direction in which the thing is seen—in the words 'the thing I see is to the east of me;' if the Eye got at the object, there could be no such notion of direction; as the perceiving organ would, in that case, be in the same place as the object; for instance, in the case of Perception by the nose, and the hand, in which the organs do actually get at, and are in touch with the objects, we have no such notion of direction. (d) A fourth reason in support of the same view is that at one and the same time the Eye apprehends near as well as remote things:

anything that has motion, when it continues to move, gets at the nearer object sooner than it does at the remoter one; whereas in the case of the Eye, we find that we see the branches of the tree, which is close to us, at the same time as we see the moon beyond the branches, which is far off from us; all which goes to prove that the Eye has no motion; and having no motion, it cannot get at objects."

In answering these the *Vārṭika* takes the arguments *seriatim*: (a) It has been argued that the eye does not get at its object, because we see things at a distance from ourselves. Now what is meant by the object being at a distance? If it means that the object is not in touch with our body, then the premises put forward as containing the reason becomes identical with what is sought to be proved; as in that case, the argument would simply mean 'the eye does not get at the object, because the object is not in touch with it;' which is the same thing as to say that 'the eye is not in touch with the object because it is not in touch with it.' If by a thing being perceived at a distance it be meant that the thing is perceived *along with the distance*,—then we ask, what is this 'distance' that is perceived? Is *it ākāsha?* or mere negation? or some other substance? If it is *ākāsha*, then it can never be perceived by the eye, being absolutely colourless. If then, 'distance' be regarded as some other substance having colour, then, inasmuch as a coloured substance can never be transparent, such an intervening substance would act as an obstruction to the perception of the object beyond; and hence there could be no perception of the object along with a coloured substance, in the shape of *distance*. If lastly by 'distance' be meant mere negation (absence of all things), then it has to be borne in mind that it is a well-recognised fact that whenever negation is perceived, it is perceived only as related to something else, and not independently by itself; so in this case the perception of a thing at a distance would involve the perception of the thing, as also the perception of the negation of a particular thing or things,—which is never found to be the case. Then again, the argument is sometimes taken to mean 'because we have the perception of things in the form *this is remote from me.*' But this idea is due to causes very much different from the eye not getting at the object: It is with reference to our body that we regard things as near or remote from us; and the idea is not due to the thing being got at or nor got at by the sense-organ concerned. In a case where the body and the sense-organ are both in touch with the object, we regard it as *near;* and when the object is related only to the organ, and is not in touch with the body, it is regarded as *remote.* Thus then, the perception of a thing as *remote* being due to the absence of touch with our body, it cannot be accepted as a proof for the eye not getting at the object. (b) The second reason propounded in support of the view that the Eye does not get at its object is that it apprehends things larger than itself. There is not much force in this: all that is necessary for the bringing about of perception is some sort of contact between the sense-organ and the object; so that it is not necessary for the entire thing in all its parts to be in contact with the eye; it is enough if the object is in contact with some parts of the organ, or the organ is in contact with some parts of the object. And as for the Eye apprehending things of varying sizes, the explanation is simple. The connection of the Eye with distant objects is possible only through the light emanating from the Eye touching the object; and just as in the case of the lamp and other sources of light, though the light is originally collected round the wick only, yet when it goes out, it moves out in gradually expanding circles and thereby lightens objects of varying sizes; in the same manner in the case of the Eye, the light originally collected within the ball, moves out of the eye in gradually expanding circles, and thereby renders perceptible objects of varying sizes. And thus it becomes possible for the Eye to get at and apprehend things larger than itself. (c) The third argument put forward was that we often speak of the direction in which the thing is perceived. As a matter of fact however, this mention of direction is with reference to the body, and not to the sense-organ; as a matter of fact, in cases where the organ and the rest of the body are both in contact with the object perceived, there is neither any mention of direction, nor any idea of the thing being near or remote; when however the object is in contact with the organ only, and not with the rest of the body, then alone have we such notions as those of direction, proximity or remoteness,—all these notions thus being relative to the body, and dependent upon the largeness or smallness of the number of conjunctions of the sense-organ, which is in contact with an object, with the points of space intervening between the object and the body; for instance, when I see a cow, I regard it as *near* when the points of space between the cow and my body are few, and *remote* when these points are many. (d) The fourth argument adduced is that we see the branch of the tree, which is near us, at the same time that we see the distant moon. This also is not sound; as what is cited is not true; we do not see the branch and the moon at the same time; the seeing is not quite simultaneous; the idea of simultaneity is due to our not perceiving the very minute interval of time that passes after our seeing of the branch and before our seeing of the moon; it is true that the time is very short; but that there is some little interval cannot be denied; the time taken by the visual light to reach the moon must be longer than that taken to reach the tree. Then again, if the Eye were operative without getting at the object, and if it were not necessary for the Eye to go up to the object, before apprehending it, any obstruction of vision would be impossible; the Eye would be able to apprehend things behind the wall just as well as the thing directly before it. If, on the other hand, it is necessary for the Eye to get at the object, then obstruction becomes possible; for in accordance with this view, what is meant by the Eye getting at the object is the falling upon the object of the light emanating from the Eye; and so when there is a wall between the Eye and the object, the light proceeding from the Eye would naturally be intercepted by the wall, and the vision obstructed. Similarly with remote objects, their non-perception can be accounted for only by the fact that the light from the Eye is unable to reach that distance; if it were not necessary for the Eye to reach its object, the non-perception of very remote objects could not be explained.

It having been proved that no arguments are tenable in support of the view that the Eye does not get at objects, the *Vārṭika* proceeds to propound positive proofs in support of the view that the Eye does get at objects: The Eye must operate by getting at the object, because it is a sense-organ, like the nose; in every-day experience we find that the organs of touch and smell—the hand and the nose—actually reach their objects before these are perceived; and in the absence of any reasons to the contrary, we can assert the same of the organ of vision, the Eye, also. It may be that the Opponent may deny the actual approach in the case of the hand and nose also; in that case we shall state our argument in a more generalised form,—'The sense-organs, to be operative, must reach their objects, because they are instruments, like the axe;' as a matter of fact, in ordinary life whenever we find an instrument operating upon an object, we find it actually reaching, coming into direct touch with, the object; *e.g.* when the axe cuts, when the stick of the potter touches the clay to make the jar, and so forth; and as the sense-organs, in bringing about cognitions, are only instruments, there is no reason why they should not get at their objects. We go a step further, and assert that causes of all kinds—and not instruments only—stand in need of such aids as the getting at objects and so forth; for if causes were to bring about their effects irrespective of such aids, and entirely through their own inherent potency, then all effects would be produced at all places and at all times; as there can be no time at which the cause is not present in some place or another. Thus then, the conclusion is that all causes—the potter's stick, the sense-organs and all—are operative when they get at their objects. Even such imperceptible causes as Ḍharma and Aḍharma are operative only when they get at the Soul in which their effects are produced in the form of pleasure and pain—says the *Nyāyamañjarī* (p. 479).

Perception, the *Sūṭra* tells us, is produced by the contact of the sense-organ. This 'contact' is of six kinds: *viz.* (1) conjunction, (2) inherence in that which is in conjunction, (3) inherence in that which inheres in that which is in conjunction, (4) inherence, (5) inherence of the inherent, and (6) qualification. To exemplify these (1) when we see the jar, the jar endowed with a certain colour is the 'object,' and the Eye the 'sense-organ;' and the 'contact' of these two is in the form of *Conjunction;* as both are material substances, and as such capable of mutual conjunction; (2) when we perceive the colour of the orange, or the motion of the cart, the contact of the Eye with the colour or with the moving cart cannot be in the form of conjunction, as Colour or Motion is not a material substance; the contact in this case is in the form of *inherence in that which is in conjunction with the Eye,* the Colour inhering in the orange which is in Conjunction with the Eye, and the Motion inhering in the cart which is in conjunction with the Eye; (3) when we perceive the genus to which the Colour belongs, the contact with the Eye is in the form of *inherence in that which inheres in that which is in conjunction with the Eye,*—the genus inhering in the colour, which inheres in the orange, which is in conjunction with the Eye; (4) when we perceive sound, the contact with the auditory organ is in the form of direct *inherence,*—the sound inhering in the *Ākāsha* of the auditory organ, this organ being only *Ākāsha* as enclosed under the ear-cavity; (5) when we perceive the genus to which a certain sound belongs, the contact is in the form of *inherence of the inherent,*—the genus inhering in Sound, which inheres in the *Ākāsha* of the auditory organ; (6) when we perceive Inherence and Negation, the contact is in the form of the qualification of that which is in conjunction,—inherence being the qualification of the inherent object which is in conjunction with the perceiving organ, and Negation, according to the Logician, being the qualification of the spot of Earth which is in conjunction with the organ. Thus we find that the Sūṭra has introduced the word 'contact' because it includes all those conditions that give rise to perception; and this 'contact' is regarded as the distinguishing feature of Perception; as it is this that is peculiar to the causal agency that brings about perception.

The *Taṭṭvachinṭāmaṇi* (pp. 574-75) makes a distinction between the perception of the *negation of sound* and that of Inherence on the one hand, and that of the *negation of jar* on the other. In the latter that which is perceived is the qualification of what is in conjunction with the sense-organ; but in the case of the Negation of Sound, as Sound is itself a quality of the Akāsha that constitutes the auditory organ, what is perceived is itself the qualification of the perceiving organ.

It has been pointed out above that the perception of colour is due to the contact, with the sense-organ, of that in which the Colour inheres. This applies, apparently, to the case of Odour and such other qualities also. Against this the objection is raised (*Taṭṭvachinṭāmani,* p. 594) that this 'inherence in that which is in conjunction' cannot account for the perception of Colour &c.; as it is neither *conjunction* nor *inherence*, and as both of these are not present either in the sense-organ or in the Colour. The answer given to this is that what has been said to be the basis of perception is only a form of indirect connection; it cannot be denied that when the sense-organ is in direct contact with a substance, there is some sort of connection with the organ and the qualities of that substance; and it is only this connection that has been called 'inherence in what is in conjunction.'

Against the aforesaid explanation of the perception of sound—which has been held to be due to the inherence of the sound in the *Ākāsha,* which constitutes the Ear—the objection is urged that if the Ear were to perceive Sound because it inheres in *Ākāsha,* then as *all* Sounds inhere in *Ākāsha,* every person would be able to hear *all sounds;* as Ākāsha is one and indivisible; and if a particular Sound be held to inhere in the space enclosed within the man's ear-cavity,—then this would militate against the view that all sound inheres in Ākāsha. The answer to this (p. 612) is that the proximity of the Sound to the perceiving organ is assumed only on the basis of its being perceived; so that we can assume the proximity of only that sound which is actually perceived, and not of *all* sounds; and further, the inherence of the sound perceived is also in connection with the Akāsha enclosed in the ear-cavity. It is this limited inherence of sound that justifies such assertions as 'this sound is produced *here,* and that sound *there;*' if all sounds belonged to the entire *Ākāsha,* no such assertion would be possible; and it is for these reasons that Sound has been regarded to be a quality that subsists in only a portion of its substratum, and does not pervade over its entire whole.

Against the explanation of the perception of Negation provided above, there is the objection that Negation, not being a positive object, can never be in contact with any sense-organ; so that it can never be perceived by the senses. It must be regarded as cognised by means of a distinct means of cognition, to which the name 'Non-apprehension' is given. This view has been already dealt with above; where we have discussed the exact number of Pramāṇas to be admitted.

It has been rightly argued *(Taṭṭvachinṭāmaṇi,* p. 718) that if this विशेषणतासम्बन्ध were not postulated as the basis of perception of negation, it would be necessary to posit an infinite series of relations; that of negation with that relation; of that relation to another relation, and so on *ad infinitum;* as it is found in the case of *samavāya* and *samavāyin*, in which case the infinite regress is inevitable. But in the case of negation it can be avoided by the postulating of the विशेषणता-relation as the basis of the perception of negation.

Gaṅgēsha Upāḍhyāya (Ṭa. Chi., p. 720) remarks that over and above the six kinds of contact of the sense-organ with the object, what is essential in certain cases of perception is the contact or presence of light also; but the contact of the light should be with the object perceived, and not with the organ; as even though the Eye is in full light, if the object is in the dark, there is no perception; whereas when the Eye is in the dark, and the object in light, it is easily seen. This leads to the conclusion that the light-contact of the object, and not that of the organ, is essential for Perception. And what manifests the presence of light is some apparent colour; as it is only when there is some colour manifest that we are cognisant of the presence of light, not otherwise; and the presence of colour in the light is aided in its operation by the manifested colour in the object, especially as this latter bears testimony to the presence of colour in the light. As a matter of fact we find that some very massive objects,—in the shape of fragrance wafted by the wind, the massive heat of the atmosphere and so forth—are not perceived by us; and the only reason for this non-perception lies in the fact that all the causal factors necessary for this perception are not present, some essential factor is wanting; and this factor must subsist in the odour, or in the colour; and the only such factor must consist in the *manifestation* of the odour or the colour; we fail to perceive the massive heat of the atmosphere with our eyes because the colour of that heat, even though present, is not manifest; similarly we fail to perceive the massive odour of the wind, because the odour, though present, is not manifest;—similarly in the case of other massive qualities. An interesting objection is raised—"We grant that manifested Colour is the cause of perception. But how is it that we do not have the visual perception of heat in the heated frying-pan, where the colour of the fire over which the pan is heated is quite manifest. Similarly when a jar is sunk in water, and is seen with the Eye, there should be a perception also of the Sun's rays manifesting the jar; as the colour of the jar is quite manifest, and when the pan and the jar are in broad daylight there is no obstacle in the way of the perception." The answer to this (Ṭa. Chi., p. 727) is that in the case of the jar in the water, the light in the water *is* actually seen; one feels as if he did not see the light, because he cannot differentiate the whiteness of the light from the whiteness of the water through which it passes. In the case of the heated frying-pan on the other hand, the heat that is produced in the pan is quite distinct from the heat of the fire in the oven; it is a heat whose colour is not manifest, only its touch is manifest; the colour of this heat we find manifested in very rare cases, when, for instance, we find flames rising out of over-heated oil. So that in the perception of the heat of the frying-pan, its perception is by touch only; and its hot touch is quite manifest. Nor will this make the perception of brightness impossible, on the ground that there is no feeling of heat or cold in regard to brightness; brightness will always be perceived as a quality of fire; and fire will be perceived by its heat. Thus the conclusion is that in the case of every perception there should be the manifestation of that specific quality which forms the basis of the organ concerned—in visual perception, the manifestation of colour, in tactile perception the manifestation of heat or cold, in olfactory perception the manifestation of odour, in auditory perception the manifestation of Sound.

(B) We shall now take up the second qualification of Perception, as defined by the Sūtra: *'it is not expressed by words.'*

The *Bhāṣya* says—Some people have held the view that there is no such perception as is entirely free from verbal representation; this view may be briefly put as follows: "As many things there are in this world so many also are the names or words expressive of them; and through these names, the things come to be cognised as identical with, or inseparable from, the words; and it is on such cognition that all usage is based; that is to say, every cognition of objects that is produced by the contact of the sense-organs is in the form of 'colour' or 'taste' &c.'; all these words are names of objects, by which names the cognition is expressed in such words as—'such and such a person perceives colour,' 'such other perceives taste,' and so on; and that which is thus expressed by means of names must be inseparable from, and always accompanied by, words; whence it follows that there is no perception that is free from verbal representation." The sense of this objection has been thus explained in the *Ṭāṭparya*—"Every object has a name; there is nothing that is devoid of name; this establishes the identity of the thing with its name; the name cannot be regarded as the *means* of the thing; whenever we perceive a thing—a cow for instance,—we perceive it as 'this is a cow,' where there is distinct co-ordination between the thing 'this' and its name 'cow,' both being in the same case; if the name were the *means*, the expression would be 'this is *by the cow*'; things thus being identical with their names, there can be no perception entirely devoid of verbal expression. This does not mean that the cognition is actually *verbal*, produced by words; what it means is that it is inseparably connected with verbal expression."

It is in view of the above, continues the *Bhāṣya*, that the author of the *Sūtra* has added the qualification that perception should *not be expressible by words*. In a case where the relation of the object with a word is not known,—*i.e.*, when we do not know the name of the object that we perceive—the apprehension of the object that there is certainly never spoken of by means of any name; and even when the relation is known, it is known in the form 'such is the name of the thing I perceive,' where the two are entirely distinct, and not identical. Even when the name of a thing is known, the cognition of the thing itself does not differ from that cognition of it which we have when its name is not known; and whenever the name is mentioned, this notion of the name appears only as an additional factor superadded on to the apprehension of the thing itself,—this apprehension, by itself, remaining as before, entirely independent of all idea of the name. Where the use of the name lies is only in the communicating of the apprehension to others: So long as there is no appellation or verbal expression for the cognition of an object, it cannot be mentioned to others, and thereby put to any practical use. Thus whenever the cognition of things is described in words, the name of the object is preceded by the preposition *'iti,'* 'as;' the form in which the cognition is described being 'the thing is cognised *as* colour, रूपमिति ज्ञायते. For these reasons we conclude that the apprehension of things brought about by their contact with sense-organs is one that is entirely free from verbal representation.

The *Vārṭika* adds that some writers have held that the qualification *avyapaḍēshya* (which we have hitherto translated as 'not expressible by *words*') has been added for the purpose of excluding inferential cognition. How this exclusion is accomplished is thus explained by the *Ṭaṭparya:* From the contact of the sense-organ with the object we infer the motion of the sense-organ; the inferential cognition of this motion is also 'produced by sense-contact;' as it is from this contact that the Inference proceeds; and it is for excluding such inferential cognitions from the category of 'Perception' that the qualification *'avyapaḍēshya'* has been added: '*apaḍēsha*' is the statement of the reason or probans; '*vyapaḍēsha,*' *vishiṣta-apaḍēsha* thus is the correct statement of the probans; and *'vyapaḍēshya,'* is that cognition which is obtained from the said correct premiss or statement of probans; and '*avyapaḍēshya*' is that cognition which does *not* follow the statement of any probans; thus *'avyapaḍēshya'* is synonymous with 'non-inferential.' This explanation of the purpose of the qualification is rejected by the *Vārṭika;* as a matter of fact, it argues, no inferential cognition is ever 'produced by the contact of the sense-organ with the object;' hence this latter qualification being sufficient for the purpose of excluding inferential cognition, any further qualification cannot be needed for that purpose.

We have seen what the oldest works, the *Bhāṣya* and the *Vārṭika* have got to say on the subject. But a very full discussion of the question is found in the *Nyāyamañjarī* (pp. 77-86). We shall now see what we can learn from this of the various views that have been held on this subject.

In seeking to prove the reality of the external world, the Logician has to adhere to the view that words denote real entities, and not mere negations; and the logical outcome of this view is that every thing in the world has one or more words related to it; it therefore will often happen that the cognition that we have of things has some word or words entering into it; it is with a view to exclude such cognitions that the word '*avyapaḍēshya*' has been added.

The older Logicians, including the author of the *Bhāṣya,* have held that the term serves to exclude such cognitions as 'this is colour,' 'this is taste,' and the like, which are expressed in words forming the names of real entities. This view may not be accepted, says Jayanṭa Bhatta. A cognition does not lose its validity, its *prāmāṇya,* simply because it is expressed in words forming the names of things. If the cognition 'this is colour' represents a fact—if what is seen is really colour, and nothing else—and if we are not in any doubt as to its being seen as such,—we can have no justification for rejecting the cognition as invalid. And as for those cognitions that do not represent real facts, they are excluded by the qualification "*avyabhichāri,' not erroneous,* in the definition. And if the cognition 'this is colour' is valid, it must be Perception, it cannot be inferential or verbal or analogical. Though this view of the *Bhaṣya* is thus criticised here, this is the conclusion that has been ultimately accepted as the most acceptable (*Nyāyanañjarī* p. 87).

A writer spoken of as 'Āchārya' by the *Nyāyamañjarī* (p. 78), and described in the footnote as Vāchaspaṭi Mishra [though the passage is not found in his *Ṭāṭparyaṭīkā,* the work specified in the footnote], has held the view that the qualification 'not expressible by words' is added for excluding that cognition of things where its name enters as an integral factor; for instance, a man sees a fruit, and not knowing its name, he is told by a trustworthy person that it is a jack-fruit; then the cognition that he ultimately has is in the form 'this is a jack-fruit;' now this cognition, so far as the cognition of the fruit is concerned, is sense-born; but as regards the name, it is purely verbal, being produced by the assertion of a trustworthy person; hence being partly *sensuous* and partly *verbal,* it cannot be regarded as 'perception.' The later writers have objected to this view on the ground that this cognition being valid, must be either perceptional or verbal; it cannot be neither.

According to these later writers, the qualification has been 'added with a view to save the definition from becoming impossible.' The Logician's opponent holds that there is no such thing as purely sense-born cognition, every cognition involving the name of the object cognised, and thus being verbal; thus there being no such thing as 'Sensuous Perception,' any definition of it is impossible; and it is with a view to meet this view that the Sūṭra has added the qualification 'not expressible by words.' It cannot be denied that in every case of Perception, before any idea of the name of the cognised object comes up, there is a cognition of the object, entirely free from any verbal expression; and it is this pure cognition that is meant to be included under the name 'Perception.' So that according to this view it is only the *Nirvikalpaka* or Non-determinate Cognition of the thing–in itself without any notion of its name or any qualities of it,– that is 'Perception;' from which name the *Savikalpaka* or Determinate Cognition becomes excluded.

This view is not countenanced by the 'Āchāryas': We cannot exclude from 'Perception' such cognitions as 'this is a cow' when we find them brought about by the contact of the object (cow) with our sense-organs; and the mere fact of one factor of it partaking of the name that happens to be remembered at the time cannot make the cognition cease to be *sense-born Perception.* The purpose of the qualification 'not expressible by words' therefore must be to exclude only such cognitions as are due to both sense-contact and trustworthy assertion.

The upshot of the whole discussion is this–The *Savikapaka* or Determinate Perception constituting the very life of the Logician, he can never regards as 'verbal' those cognitions that are brought about by the joint instrumentality of sense-contact and words. As to whether a certain particular cognition is to be regarded as *sensuous* or *verbal,* it will depend upon what relationship of the cognition is actually recognised at the time; so that in the case of the cognition 'this is a cow,' the whole burden cannot rest upon the *word* 'cow' only. It is best therefore to accept the view of the *Bhāṣya* that the qualification 'not expressible by words' serves to exclude only those cognitions which are described by means of words; I perceive the cow,–this is perception; but when I describe this perception to another person 'I am perceiving a cow,' this becomes purely verbal: And it is the cognition produced by such descriptions that are meant to be excluded by the qualification in question. Thus

Savikalpaka and *Nirvikalpaka* are both included under 'Perception;' with only this difference that in the former the perception is aided by such accessory causes as the remembrance of the name and the idea of the properties of the thing; while in the *Nirvikalpaka*, the perception is due entirely to sense-contact, independently of all accessories.

(C) We shall now take up the third qualification of Perception as defined by the Sūṭra—'*which is not erroneous.*'

Says the *Bhāṣya*—"During the summer it often happens that the sun's rays become mixed up with the heat-rays radiating from the Earth's surface; and the two together flickering at a distance come into contact with the eye of the observer, who apprehends the flickering mass as *water*. Now, if the definition of Perception consisted of only two terms—'that which is produced by sense-object contact,' and 'that which is not representable by words,'—then the apprehension of 'water' under the above circumstances would have to be regarded as real 'Perception.' With a view to guard against this contingency, the author has added the further qualification that the cognition should be 'not-erroneous.' That cognition is 'erroneous' in which a thing is apprehended as what it is not; while when a thing is perceived as what it is, the Perception is 'not-erroneous'."

This qualification, Vāchaspaṭi Mishra remarks, is necessary in the definition of Perception only, and not in that of Inferential Cognition and the rest; as in the case of the latter, the erroneousness, whenever present, lies in the Perception upon which every one of them is based.

The *Vārṭika* (p. 39) raises the question—What is it that is *erroneous*? Does the error lie in the object or in the cognition? Some Naiyāyikas have held that it is in the object that the error lies; it is the object that appears, is apprehended, as what it is not; and it is on account of this wrong apprehension that the cognition is called 'erroneous.' The

Vārṭika does not accept this view. Even when the object is apprehended as what it is not, it, by itself, remains actually what it is; *e.g.* when in regard to the flickering rays there arises the cognition of 'water,' there is no error in the rays: the rays do not become not-rays, nor the flickering not-flickering; the flickering rays remain flickering rays; the error lies in those rays being cognised as what they are not, as *water;* so that what is actually the 'apprehension of the flickering rays' appears as the 'apprehension of water;' it is the apprehension which appears as what it is not; hence what the error lies in is the apprehension or cognition, and not the object.

(D) The fourth qualification of Perception mentioned in the *Sūṭra* is 'which is well-defined.'

The *Bhāṣya* explains this as follows: 'When the man looks from a distance, and sees something rising from the earth, the cognition that he has is in the doubtful form—'this is smoke, or dust;'—inasmuch as this doubtful cognition is also 'produced by the sense-object contact,' it would have to be regarded as 'Perception,' if this were defined simply as 'that cognition which is produced by the sense-object contact.' With a view to guard against this the author has added the further qualification that the cognition should be 'well-defined.'

Against the above, the following objection has been raised: "The qualification cannot be taken as serving the purpose of excluding doubtful cognition: because as a matter of fact doubtful cognition is not 'produced by sense-object contact;' it is due entirely to the mind;—the very name '*samshaya,*' derived from the root *shī,* to lie down, with the upasarga "*sam,*" denotes *cogitation based upon a particular character;* and this cogitation consists in the attributing of two mutually contradictory characters, recalled to the Mind, to a single substratum; hence in a doubtful cognition, all that the

Sense-organ does is to present before the mind that one substratum; and all the rest of the process of the cogitation—the recalling of the diverse characters, and the attributing of these to the perceived substratum—is the work of the mind; hence doubtful cognition must be regarded as a purely mental product."

As a matter of fact however, as the *Bhāṣya* remarks, doubtful cognitions are produced, not always by the Mind alone, but by both: some are produced by the contact of the Mind with the Soul, while others are produced by the contact of the object with the sense-organ; and what the qualification 'well-defined' is meant to exclude is only that doubtful cognition which is produced by the sense-object contact; as it is only such cognition that could, as produced by the sense-object contact, have any chance of being regarded as Perception. In fact the case of Doubtful Cognition is on a par with that of Representative Cognition, *Anuvyavasāya*: in all cases of Perception, the sense-organ of the perceiver is always operative, and the operation of the mind comes in only subsequently for purposes of the representative cognition, which recalls to the mind the cognition previously got through the Senses; and just as in this representative cognition, which, though due directly to the operation of the Mind, sense-operation is essential,—so in the case of Doubtful Cognition also, which is due directly to Mind-operation, the operation of the Sense-organ is essential.

We have seen above that the later Logicians were always under the apprehension of the Sūtra being regarded as excluding the *Savikalpaka* Cognition from the category of 'Perception.' That this exclusion was intended by Gauṭama and also (perhaps) by Vāṭsayāyana and Uḍyoṭakara appears more than probable. But the later Logicians have always made it their business to argue that the definition provided by the *Sūṭra* applies to *Savikalpaka* as well as to *Nirvikalpaka*

Perception. In connection, therefore, with the qualification 'well-defined,' which is the only word in the definition that can justify this interpretation, Vāchaspaṭi Mishra, realising that if this qualification be taken as simply meaning 'certain,' and hence as excluding doubtful cognitions, there would be nothing to justify the inclusion of the *Savikalpaka* Perception, proceeds to show that Doubtful Cognition is already excluded by the qualification 'not erroneous;' for when we apprehend a thing as '*this or that,*' we do apprehend it as something that it is not; hence the qualification 'well-defined' should be taken as serving the purpose of including *Savikalpaka* cognition; so that the qualification 'not expressible by words' takes in the *Nirvikalpaka* or non-determinate Cognition, and 'well-defined' takes in the *Savikalpaka* or Determinate Cognition,—the definition thus being made applicable to both kinds of Perception (*Ṭaṭparya,* p. 84). Vāchaspaṭi Mishra seeks to justify his interpretation by the remark that the *Bhāṣya* and the *Vārṭika* have omitted to make mention of the inclusion of the *Savikalpaka* cognition, as this was a fact too plain to need an explanation; and that his explanation is based upon the view taken by an ancient writer of the name of Ṭrilochana Guru (a writer, by the way, of whom we know nothing). As a matter of fact however, the *Bhāṣya* and the *Vārṭika* do not only *not* mention the inclusion of the *Savikalpaka* cognition, but from the explanation that they provide of the Sūṭra, they make it tolerably clear that they mean the name 'Perception' to apply to *Nirvikalpaka* cognition only. It would seem therefore that the Diṅnāga's definition of Perception as '*Kalpanāpodhamabhrānṭam*' was a correct rendering of Gauṭama's meaning; and it is remarkable that in course of its vigorous attack upon this definition, the Vārṭika directs its assault entirely against the term 'Kalpanā.'

The *Nyāyamañjarī* objects to the view that Doubtful Cognition is excluded by the qualification 'not-erroneous.' It remarks that Doubtful Cognition is entirely different from

Erroneous Cognition; and as such could not be excluded by the qualification 'not-erroneous.' It must, therefore, be taken as excluded by the last qualification 'well-defined.'

With regard to this last qualification, there is a point that deserves consideration. The definition contains the word '*vyavasāyāṭmakam.*' May this not be taken as excluding the *Anuvyavasāya,* or representative Cognition, which, according to the Logician, accompanies every cognition? This is thrown out only as a suggestion; and we desist from further comment.

With regard to the Sūṭra's definition of Perception, the *Vārṭika* raises the question as to whether the definition propounded is to be taken piece-meal, or as one complete whole. That is, are the qualifications to be taken as each individually providing an all-sufficient definition of Perception, or all of them collectively? This doubt arises from the fact that Gauṭama, in his Sūṭras, has provided both kinds of definition; for instance, in Sū. 1-1-10 we read—'Desire, Effort, Aversion, Pleasure, Pain and Cognition are the characteristics of the Self,' wherein each of the six factors mentioned has been held to constitute singly a sufficient definition of the Self; so also in the definition of Doubt provided in Sū. 1-2-23;—while Sū. 1-2-10 defines Casuistry as 'the subversion of the assertions made by the other party by means of suppositions',—where the whole constitutes the necessary definition; so also in Sū. 1-1-6, where Analogy is defined as that which 'accomplishes the desired end by means of similarity to something that is well known'—where the whole forms a single definition. Thus there is sufficient ground for raising the question as to the exact signification of the definition of Perception.

The answer to the question is that the words of the Sūṭra are to be taken collectively as affording a single definition of Perception; and this for the simple reason that each of the qualifications severally serves to exclude Inferential Cognition, Pleasure and Pain, Verbal Cognition, Wrong Cognition and Doubtful Cognition; under the circumstances, if every one of the five words were to constitute a distinct definition, then, by turns, Inferential Cognition and the rest would come to be regarded as 'Perception;' for instance, if we took out the first qualification–'produced by sense-object contact'–and accepted the rest of it as the complete definition of Perception, such a definition would be applicable to Inferential Cognition, which fulfils all the other conditions except that it is not brought about by the contact of the sense-organ with the object cognised; and so on. Thus all the thirty definitions that could be formed by the dropping of one or more of the five factors of the definition, being found defective, the entire Sūṭra should be taken as affording only one definition.

Why should the definition of Perception contain the word '*jñāna*,' 'cognition?'

The answer is simple enough: because every definition must proceed with stating the genus to which the thing belongs, and then indicating the features that distinguish it from other members of the same genus; and Perception belongs to the genus 'cognition,' and is distinguished from other cognitions by being produced by sense-object contact and so forth. But the *Vārṭika* on p. 38 finds a deeper purport in the word: It is introduced for the purpose of excluding Pleasure and such other things, which also, as produced by the contact of the sense-organs with the object, have to be excluded.

Though such is the view expressed on p. 38, we find the *Vārṭika* on p. 41 speaking of 'the cognition of pleasure' as 'produced by sense-object contact;' the *Bhāṣya* on p. 16 actually includes '*sukhāḍi,*' 'Pleasure and the rest,' under

'Perception.' What then would be the point in excluding Pleasure from the definition of 'Perception?'—asks the Bauḍḍha Logician. It is true that in the production of the 'cognition of pleasure' there enter some more factors than in ordinary Perception; as the *Ṭāṭparya* remarks (on p. 81, II. 6-8 and 27-28); but that cannot justify the exclusion of the cognition from 'Perception.' Reading the two passages of the *Vārṭika* (on p. 38 and 41) together, we are led to believe that a distinction is made between 'Pleasure' and 'Cognition of Pleasure.' But what is *pleasure* apart from the feeling of agreeableness? And certainly this feeling is a form of *Cognition.* It may be that in some cases the Pleasure, even though present, may not be actually *felt*; but such is the case with all cognitions. The *Ṭāṭparya* on p. 81, Ils. 6-8, also declares *'sukhāḍayaḥ...mānasapraṭyakṣavēḍanīya iṭi ramaṇiyām.'* So the attempt to exclude Pleasure and Pain from 'Perception' can be justified only on making a distinction between 'Pleasure' and 'Cognition of Pleasure:' Pleasure being regarded as the *object* perceived, and not the cognition itself; hence as colour, being distinct from colour-perception, cannot be included under 'Perception,' so also pleasure, being distinct from pleasure-cognition, cannot be included under 'Perception.' Pleasure—*i.e.,* agreeable feeling or sensation—is produced by the proximity of a thing that we desire; for instance, a nice cool wind may be blowing, and actually producing the agreeable sensation of coolness; so that the pleasure is there; but there is no 'cognition' of this pleasure until the mind is brought into contact with the sensation; so that the agreeable sensation of coolness is produced by the tactile contact of the skin with the cool wind—the contact, that is, of the organ of touch with the object,—but it is not Perception, as it is not *cognition* until the operation of the mind comes in; and when this comes, there is *cognition* of the agreeable sensation; and as this is a *cognition,* and is produced by the contact of the organ of mind with the object, in the shape of the agreeable sensation,—it falls under 'Perception.'

The definition of Perception given in the Sūṭra as the right cognition produced by the contact of the object with the sense-organ, has been rejected by the modern Naiyāyikas. Their reason is three-fold: Firstly, this definition applies to all right cognitions; as every cognition is produced by the contact of the object with the mind, and the mind is a sense-organ; secondly the definition does not apply to the perception that God has of all things; as the perceptions of God do not stand in need of any sense-contact; thirdly, what is a 'sense-organ' can be determined only by Perception; so that the introduction of this word into the definition involves a vicious circle.

Gaṅgēsha Upāḍhyāya offers his own definition of Perception as being a *cognition not having a cognition for its instrument; i.e.* a cognition not produced by the instrumentality of cognition. (Ṭaṭṭvachintāmaṇi, p. 552). Every other kind of cognition has a cognition for its instrument, or most efficient cause: For instance, the instrument of Inferential Cognition consists in the cognition of the invariable concomitance of the probans and the probandum and that of the presence of the probans in the subject; and Verbal Cognition has for its instrument the cognition of the meaning of words; Analogical Cognition is produced by the cognition of similarity. But in the producing of Perception, we do not have the instrumentality of any cognition; the sense-organs being the only instrument concerned,—as the *Māṭhurī* points out. Similarly also in the case of Recognition—'this that I see is the same as that which I had seen'—the instrumentality of the remembrance of 'that which I had seen' is essential; and as remembrance also is a form of 'cognition' the definition suggested cannot apply to it. God's perception, not being produced by any instrumentality, can be regarded as *not having cognition for its instrument*, and thus included in the definition.

The later Naiyāyikas do not accept this definition either. Thoroughgoing Theists as they are, they hold that every event in this world is produced by the wish of God; so that every cognition–Perception included–that we have is *produced by the cognition* of God; and thus the definition 'that which is not produced by the instrumentality of cognition' cannot apply to any cognition at all. But, as is their practice, they do not reject the definition suggested by their *Āchārya* Gaṅgēsha; they offer an explanation of the definition, by which they avoid the difficulty that has been urged. 'What is meant by a cognition *being produced by a cognition'* says the *Māṭhurī* (p. 559), is that which is स्वावच्छिन्नकार्यता-प्रतियोगिककारणताश्रयज्ञानजन्यमात्रवृत्तिधर्मावच्छिन्नकारणताप्रत्योगिक - कार्यतावच्छेदकम्; that is, 'it is characterised by that कार्यता (character of product) which has for its corresponding cause that which is characterised by a property that subsists only in that which is produced by a cognition which is the substratum of the causal character which corresponds to the product-character characterised by the cognition in question.' For instance, in the case of Inferential Cognition we find that 'the cognition which is the substratum of the causal character corresponding to that cognition' is *the cognition of invariable concomitance,*–and what is 'produced' by this is *the cognition of the subsistence in the subject, of the probans as concomitant with the probandum,*–and that which is characterised by a property subsisting in this only is the cause of which the Inferential Cognition is the effect. And the qualification 'that which is produced' serves to preclude God's cognitions, which are never *produced;* so that even if Perception is produced by God's cognition, it becomes excluded from this.

Having supplied a definition of Perception in Sū. 1. 1.4, Gauṭama proceeds to consider the nature of Perception in greater detail, in Sū. 2. 1. 20 to 36. Sūṭras 20–25 raise the question as to why the definition of Perception does not make mention of 'the contact of the Mind and the Soul' which is accepted by all to be essential in all cognitions. Mind-Soul contact, it is urged, is as good as cause of Perception as the 'sense-object contact.' Similarly with Space and Time, both of which are necessary for Perception, there can be no Perception except at some time and place. Time and Place also, therefore, should be regarded as essential causes of Perception, and as such, should be mentioned in the Sūṭra. There is some confusion as to the distribution of these Sūṭras between *Pūrvapakṣa* and *Siḍḍhānta;* for which see Translation of *Sūṭra* with *Bhāṣya* and *Vārṭika,* in loco.

Su. 25 to 29 supply the answer to this objection: The Mind-Soul contact is a factor that is common to all forms of cognition; and as such need not appear in the definition of Perception, which can and should mention only those factors that, being peculiar to Perception, serve to distinguish it from all other forms of cognition; and the only contact that is so peculiar is the Sense-object Contact, which, on that account, finds a place in the Sūṭra. Another reason why the Sense-object contact is more important, in the matter of Perception, than every other contact, lies in the fact that when a man is asleep, if a loud sound is produced near him, or when he is roughly handled, he wakes up,—which is due only to the contact between the Sound and his auditory organ; or to that between the handling and his tactile organ, and the other contact, that of the Mind and Soul, may be regarded as almost absent in this case; as Soul-Contact can be brought about only by an effort put forth by the Soul, and in the case of the sleeping man, there can be no much conscious effort, and the mind is also either dormant, or taken up by certain dreaming-cognitions that the man may be passing through at the time; and so the Mind-Soul contact, even though present, could not be strong enough to bring about the waking perception. This proves that it is the Sense-object contact that is more prominent factor in the cause of Perception than the Mind-

Soul contact. Sū. 27 provides another argument: as a matter of fact we find that every perception is named either after its object or after the sense-organ concerned—when we hear a sound, we call it either the 'perception of sound' or 'auditory perception;' when we see the colour of an object we call it either 'the perception of colour,' or 'visual perception;' and we never call it either 'mental perception' or 'soul-perception;' this shows that the sense-organ and the object, through their contact, are more important factors in the generating of Perception than any other contact.

Sū. 28 raises an objection: "If the waking cognition referred to in Sū. 26 is produced independently of Mind-soul contact,—does this mean that this contact is not necessary for any cognition at all? If so, this is a direct contradiction of those Sūṭras that have asserted the agency of the Soul and Mind towards the generating of cognitions; in fact the only important argument that has been put forward in Sū. 1. 1. 16 in support of the postulating of Mind implies that the operation of mind is essential in all cognitions. If then, with a view to avoid this contradiction, the agency of mind-soul contact be admitted in *all* cognitions, then, the necessity of mentioning this in the definition of Perception becomes quite patent."

Sū. 29 answers this objection: All that we mean is that so far as Perception is concerned, the sense-object contact is the predominant element; it does not mean that the mind-soul contact is absent or unnecessary. Both are there; and to a certain extent both are essential; but the sense-object contact is regarded as the more important of the two, and the more necessary to mention, because that is what distinguishes Perception from all other kinds of cognition. The above-mentioned waking cognition also is not entirely devoid of Soul-contact; but what is the direct cause is the forcible character of the objects—the loudness of the sound and the roughness of the handling; if these circumstances were not there, no amount of Mind or Soul contact could awaken the man.

Sū. 30 raises another question. "We need not," the opponent argues, "admit Perception as a distinct form of Cognition; it is only a particular form of Inference. In what is called the 'perception of the tree,' what is actually in contact with the perceiving eye is only a part of the tree, either the root or the trunk, or a few of its branches; and when from this we have the Cognition of the *whole* tree, it is only a case of inferring the whole by its parts; or seeing the root we have the Cognition of the entire tree, which latter is not in contact with the Eye; and this is exactly similar to the Cognition that we have of the unseen fire from the perception of smoke."

The answer to this is given in Sū. 31; but the *Bhāṣya* and the *Vārṭika* have supplied an answer under Sū. 30 also. This is as follows: It cannot be maintained that Perception is only an inference from the cognition of parts, of something different from the parts; as none of the alternatives that this view admits of is found to be tenable. For instance, what is that 'something different from the parts,' which is inferred from the cognition of the parts?

"Well, if you accept the view that the composite whole—the tree for instance—is only a conglomeration of several component particles, then the 'something different' will be those particles that, not being in contact with the Eye, are not seen;—and if you accept the other view that the composite whole is, as a whole, a substance different from its component particles, then the 'something different' will be either this composite whole, the entire tree, or those parts of it that are not perceived. In either case there being an invariable concomitance, between the perceived part with the other parts, as well as with the object as a whole, it is only natural that the cognition of the former should lead to the inference of the latter."

In answering the above the *Bhāṣya* begins with criticising the example that has been cited—the case of the perception of the tree. If the composite whole, the tree, is nothing more or less than its component parts, then there can be no perception of the 'tree' as a whole; as no such thing exists; neither the part perceived, nor the part unperceived, can be called the 'tree;' and all that is possible is that perception of one part leads us to infer the other parts that are not perceived; so that inference, if it comes, pertains only to the other parts, and not to the tree as a whole; so that it is not right to call the 'perception of the tree' *Inference*. If, on the other hand, the composite whole, the tree as a whole, is something different from the component particles, then also its apprehension cannot be 'Inference;' as this inference could be based only upon the relation of concomitance perceived between the parts and the whole; and if this relation is perceived, it means that both must be perceived; and thus the tree as a whole must be perceptible; if it were purely inferable, and never perceptible; then its relations also would be imperceptible;—*i.e.*, its concomitance with the parts would not be perceptible; and there would be no basis for the inference of the tree as a whole. Thus the cognition of the tree as a whole, in the case in question, cannot be regarded as 'inference.' In fact the composite whole being itself in direct contact with the Eye,—just as much as its parts— there is no reason why its cognition should not be regarded as pure Perception; this name would be denied to it only if the tree were absolutely an imperceptible thing; but if it were so, it would not be possible to perceive its concomitance with the parts; which would make all inference with regard to it absolutely impossible.

So much for the particular example cited of the Tree. Now as regards the general question. It has been argued that Perception is Inference; because a part of it is perceived. This is not right, says Gauṭama (Sū. 2. 1. 31), because the statement involves a self-contradiction. A part cannot be perceptible unless the whole is perceptible; hence to admit that the part is perceived, and then to deny the perceptibility of the whole involves a self-contradiction. In fact we are said to perceive the whole only when we perceive certain parts of it; we are never cognisant of *all* the parts of the thing that we perceive; in fact the cases of the tree and its parts stand on the same level; when we perceive the branch, and from that derive the cognition of the entire tree, of the branch also, we see only some parts, and not the whole; in fact there is just as much ground for regarding the cognition of the whole tree as perception as that of the parts; the whole tree is as much in contact with the Eye as the whole branch, or the whole trunk. Then again, in no case of inference is the probandum itself in contact with a sense-organ; and when we see the branch, or the trunk or the root, the entire tree is just as much in contact with the Eye as the branch and the rest; and as the cognition of the tree thus fulfils all the conditions of Perception, there can be no reason for denying the name 'Perception' to it.

Then again, as the *Ṭaṭṭvachinṭāmaṇi* (p. 584) points out, it is not true that in all Perception there is contact of the sense with a part only; for there are some perceptible objects which have no parts at all; *e.g.* the Soul. That is why it will not be right to say that Perception is brought about by the contact of the sense-organ with an appreciably large part of the object, as has been suggested by the Pūrvapakṣin (p. 581). The Opponent proposes a compromise: "The perception of the part may be due to its contact with the sense-organ; but that of the object as a whole must be due to the contact of that part which is inherent in that whole; just like the perception of Colour, which perception is due to the contact with the sense-organ of that object in which the Colour inheres." The author does not accept this compromise; and the only reason that he gives (p. 589) is that, inasmuch as in the case of one substance, Soul, we find the perception to be due to the contact of the object itself, it is more logical and much simpler to take the same view of the perception *of all substances.*

The wider question as to whether there is any such thing as a *composite whole,* has been dealt with by Gauṭama under Sūṭra 2-1-33 to 36. We shall take up this question when dealing with *the objects of cognition.*

In connection with the Logician's view that Jñāna or Cognition is perceptible as declared in *Ṭaṭṭvachinṭāmaṇi* (p. 783)—Gangesha has raised an interesting question (*Ṭaṭṭvachinṭāmaṇi,* p. 784).

It is urged that Cognition cannot be regarded as perceptible; as this would mean that the tree-perception that we have, when we see the tree, is followed by another cognition which apprehends that tree-perception; and this second cognition the Logician regards as of the nature of perception produced by mind-contact. But in the first place there is no second cognition following upon and apprehending the perception of the tree; this latter being sufficient, by itself, to form the basis of all activities pertaining to it; and under the circumstances, there can be no justification for postulating this second cognition, and then attributing it to the agency of the mind-contact. As regards the very first cognition of the tree, we have to accept the presence of this cognition, as without some such cognition, there could be no activities in regard to the tree. Such, in fact, is the position taken up by the Mīmāmsakas and the Vedantins who hold that every cognition being self-sufficient, the perception of the tree would not stand in need of any further cognition of its own; in fact, as Prabhākara, points out, in every cognition, there are three factors—the perception, the perceived thing and the perceiver; and every one of these is clearly manifest in every perception; so that there is no need of any further cognition. Specially as if every cognition stood in need of a further cognition, there would be a most undesirable 'vicious regress' in connection with every single cognition.

It might be urged in answer to this, that what is meant by a cognition being 'self-illumined' is only that so far as the cognition of its object is concerned. the cognition does not stand in need of anything else; but it does not mean that it does not stand in need of any other cognition, also in the matter of activities with regard to itself; for instance, when we speak of a cognition—when we wish to describe a certain cognition that we have had,—this mention must be made by means of words. So that even though we do not need more than one cognition, for the cognition of any particular object, yet when we come to the cognition itself, its own cognition must depend upon a further cognition; or else, if the cognition were to be the means of its own cognition, this would involve a reflexive action for which there is no proof at all. Then again, if a cognition did not give rise to further cognitions with regard to itself, how could we account for the remembrance of past cognitions? It thus cannot be denied that the perception of the tree must be itself the object of a further perception. Thus then, as a matter of fact, in every case of Perception, there would, in practice, be found involved two perceptions. For instance, one perception is in the form 'I perceive this;' and in this we have two cognitions:—*first* the cognition of 'this' (pertaining to the object perceived)—this cognition being technically called '*vyavasāya;*'—and *secondly* the cognition 'I perceive' (which pertains to the perception),—this second cognition being called *'Anuvyavasāya.'* And while the former, the cognition of 'this,' is brought about by the contact of the particular sense-organ (the Eye or the Ear, or the Nose) concerned, the latter, the cognition of the perception, is due to the contact of the Mind.

The Opponent does not accept this 'mental' perception of Cognition or of Pleasure and Pain. He argues that if every perception were necessarily followed by another perception of itself even, without the man desiring to have this second perception, then there would be no end to the series of perceptions set going by a single perception; as the contact of the mind would be always there: so that there would be no possibility of the man having any but that one cognition. It is far more reasonable therefore to accept the cognition to be self-illumined than to postulate its apprehension by another cognition and regard this latter as perceptible by means of the mind, and thereby court the aforesaid absurdities. Then as regards the difficulties that have been pointed out above, in regard to Remembrance, & c., those are easily explained. As a matter of fact, we have remembrance of only those things that have been apprehended before; and in this remembrance, the notion of 'that'—which indicates that previous apprehension—naturally enters as an essential element; and this does not at all justify the assumption of a second cognition in addition to the previous apprehension. Thus so long as we can explain all the well-known facts of experience on the basis of a single cognition 'self-illumined,' there can be no justification for the assuming of an endless series of cognitions with every cognition that we may have.

The Logician's answer to the above is as follows: The first step in the answer is the rejection of the idea that Cognition is *self-illumined*, and the second step consists in the asserting of the fact that Perception is apprehended by another Perception, which is brought about by the instrumentality of the mind (p. 797).

Perception does not vouch for the 'self-illumined' character of Cognition; as the first cognition that we have is never in the form 'I cognise;' nor does this militate against our experience; as all our activities proceed from the definite cognition of things, and not from the cognition of that cognition; and as a matter of fact, it is the first cognition that apprehends the thing; and it has nothing to do with its own apprehension; *e.g.*, when we proceed to pick up silver, this activity proceeds from the cognition 'this is silver,' and not from 'I have the perception of silver.' We do not deny this latter cognition; it does appear, but only subsequently. After the cognition 'This is silver,'—which is the first original cognition called '*vyavasāya*'—comes the second or representative cognition, 'I have the perception of silver,' which is called '*anuvyavasāya*,' and which has for its object, the corresponding *vyavasāya*.

Let us analyse the cognition 'I have the perception of silver.' Inasmuch as the perception, which is apprehended by this cognition, can never be in contact with any sense-organ, there appears in this (a) neither the function of the nominative, in which the action of knowing might inhere [as the cognition inheres in the Self; and so if the Self were to appear as the nominative, it would mean self-inherence, which is impossible], (b) nor the functioning of the objective, which consists either in bearing the effect of the action, or being the that upon which the operation of the instrument falls; (c) nor lastly, the action itself; that is to say, the cognition 'I have the perception of silver' does not imply any nominative agent, or any objective or any action; all that it implies is that the Self (the cognitive personality) has for its qualification the Cognition which in its form belongs to that category of 'cognition' which has the silver for its object; and as a matter of fact, if this cognition were self-illumined, it could not appear as a qualification; specially as the former cognition, which characterises it, could not then be known. On the other hand, if we regard the cognition 'I have the perception of silver' as a subsequent *anuvyavasāya*, this would easily appear as qualifying the Self; as its own qualification will have already appeared in the shape of the corresponding *vyāvasāya*, the perception of silver.

The self-illumined character of Cognition having been found to be untenable, it follows that it is apprehended by means of Perception. And as the only organ that can bear upon all kinds of cognitions is the Internal Organ of the Mind, we hold all cognitions to be cognisable by means of Mental Perception—*Manasa Pratyakṣa.* And we formulate our reasonings in the following syllogistic form (a) 'the sensuous perception of silver cannot apprehend itself, because it is not brought about by the contact of a sense-organ that could bring about that cognition of the perception, just as it cannot apprehend any other object that is not in contact with any sense-organ;' (b) 'a cognition that is apprehended by Perception, must be in contact with a sense-organ capable of bringing about its perception—because it is apprehended by Perception.' And as the Internal Organ is the only such organ, the inevitable conclusion is that the Cognition is apprehended by means of the contact of that Internal organ.

A fresh question is raised—Granting that the cognition 'I have the perception of silver,' the *anuvyavasāya,* is a mental perception; but it has been held that this is a qualified cognition, having for its qualification or determinant the perception of silver; from this it would follow that at the time that the *anuvyavasāya* appears the corresponding *vyavasāya,* as its qualifying determinant, should be present. This however is not possible; for every cognition has only a momentary existence; which means that at the time that the *anuvyavasāya* appears the corresponding *vyavasāya* will have ceased to exist. Under the circumstances, how can the latter be regarded as the qualifying determinant of the former? In fact, the qualification being absent, the qualified cognition, the *anuvyavasāya*—*i.e.*, the cognition in the form 'I have the perception,' becomes an impossibility.

The *Taṭṭvachinṭāmaṇi* (pp. 804-808) provides four explanations of this difficulty. (1) The qualified cognition—the *anuvyavasāya*—appears at the very moment that the qualifying *vyavasāya* is destroyed; so that once the qualifed cognition is produced, its cognition follows in due course. Specially as it is not the qualifying factor itself that is the cause of the qualified cognition; it is the cognition of the qualifying factor that is the cause; so that even after the moment at which the qualifying factor is destroyed, its cognition would be present there; and this would be sufficient for the purpose of bringing about the qualified cognition. (2) In fact what appears in the unqualified cognition—*vyavasāya*—is '*jñāna*,' as well as the generic character of '*jñanaṭva;*' so that in the *anuvyavasāya* 'I have the perception' the cognition is qualified by the generic character of '*jñanaṭva*' (which is ever existent); and the Self is qualified by the cognition. (3) This explanation is not satisfactory; for, as the *Āloka* rightly remarks, the cognition of the cognition can never be *unqualified* or *non-determinate;* as all the causal factors leading to qualified cognition are present in the case. (4) The last and the most satisfactory explanation is as follows: As a matter of fact, whenever a cognition is apprehended, it is always by means of a qualified cognition; for the cognition of cognition is always of the nature of *anuvyavasāya;* and we know that an *anuvyavasāya* is always brought about by the *vyavasāya* which is qualified or determined by its object; so that in the case of *anuvyavasāya* there are present all the causal factor necessary for qualified cognition. In fact every cognition has a dual character, being partly determinate and partly non-determinate; that which apprehends the qualifying factors is determinate, and that apprehending the mere cognition *per se,* is non-determinate. In 'I see the jar,' the *seeing* by itself is non-determinate; while the 'seeing *of the jar*' is determinate.

The 'dual character' of cognitions just mentioned brings us to the well-known division of Cognition into *Savikalpaka* or Determinate, Concrete and *Nirvikalpaka* or Non-determinate, Abstract.

Of these the Abstract, *Nirvikalpaka* Cognition is that which is entirely devoid of all *vikalpa,—i.e.,* free from all idea of the name of the thing cognised, of the category or genus to which the thing belongs,—in fact of everything that would in any way specify the thing; it is cognition of the thing merely as *something,* in a vague general sort of way.

The word '*vikalpa*' or '*kalpanā*' stands for all that specifies or limits the scope of a cognition. These Kalpanās or qualifying adjuncts have been classed under five heads (Nyā. Mañj. p. 93): (1) genus, (2) quality, (3) action, (4) name and (5) substance. When we cognise the animal before our eyes as the 'cow,' *i.e.* as belonging to the genus 'cow,' our cognition is qualified by the notion of *genus*; when we know the same animal as *white,* our cognition is qualified by the notion of a *quality;* when we see it as *walking,* our cognition is qualified by the notion of an *action*; when we recognise it as bearing a definite proper name, our cognition is qualified by the notion of that *name;* and lastly, when we know it as covered by a cloth, our cognition is qualified by the notion of the *substance,* cloth.

What proof is there of there being such an abstract or non-determinate cognition?

Kumārila Bhatta has pointed out that it is a matter of common experience that whenever we look upon a thing, the first cognition that appears in our mind is only in the vague form—'I perceive something;'—this vague cognition being exactly like the cognition that the new-born infant has when its eyes fall upon anything; and it is only after this undefined cognition has appeared that it is followed by the defined concrete cognition 'I see the cow.' All the older philosophers have contented themselves by relying upon our own experience only as the proof for Abstract Cognition. But we find that the *Taṭṭvachinṭāmaṇi,* p. 817, &c., seeks to provide regular arguments in support of this view.

The first perception that we have in the form 'this is a cow' is a qualified cognition *i.e.,* the cognition of the individual animal as characterised by a definite class-character; and as such it must be held to be produced by the cognition of that qualifying class-character 'cow', which latter cognition in its turn, is produced by something else; just as the Inferential cognition, which is the cognition of the 'Subject' as qualified by the Probandum, is produced by a previous cognition of that Probandum. That cognition of the qualification (*f.i.* the specific class-character) also cannot be regarded as a *qualified cognition;* as any such postulate would involve in infinite regress; and also because as a matter of fact cognition apprehends the class-character, pure and simple, without any idea of its either qualifying anything else, or of itself having any other qualification; and thus being a purely unqualified qualification, it must be regarded as '*nirvikalpaka*', 'abstract' or 'non-determinate;' specially as when we perceive the cow, all the notion that we have is that it is a *cow–i.e.* it is characterised by the class-character 'cow;' and there is not the slightest conception of anything further in regard to this class-character. Thus the conclusion is that in a case where there is no cognition of any qualifications–and where there is nothing that could bring about such a cognition,–*e.g.* in the case of the cow, we have nothing, at the time that we see a particular cow, to help us to know any particulars of the entire genus 'cow'–the cognition that we have in this unqualified form cannot but be regarded as 'abstract.' And as every cognition that is brought about by another cognition, must be a qualified cognition, the unqualified cognition must be held to be *a cognition not brought about by another cognition;* and this is our definition of *Perception,* which includes Abstract Cognition under the category of 'Perception.' In regard to every cognition, it has been held that, *as cognition* it is 'abstract;' it becomes 'concrete' only when we come to its object, which, if qualified, makes the cognition 'concrete,' and if unqualified, makes it remain 'abstract.' And further, as every *anuvyavasāya* or representative cognition is the product of a previous cognition, the object must appear therein as the qualification; so that, inasmuch as every cognition must be followed by the corresponding representative cognition, it follows that while every cognition, so far as the first cognition is concerned, may be either 'abstract' or 'concrete,'—it must, so far as the representative cognition is concerned, be 'concrete.' Even the ordinary cognition of the cow, is 'abstract' in so far as the conception of the class-character 'cow' is concerned; but in itself—in the form 'this is a cow'—it is 'concrete,' as its object is the individual animal *qualified* by the particular class-character. It is on account of this admixture of the two characters of 'abstract' and 'concrete,' both of which may be attributed to one and the same cognition—that those two have not been held to constitute distinct 'species;' as all *species* must be mutually exclusive.

The existence of Abstract Cognition having been proved, the Logician proceeds to discuss the question of what forms the object of that Cognition. The *Nyāyamañjarī* (p. 97 *et. seq.*) points out the difference of opinion that there has been on this subject, among the several philosophers.

(a) The Bauḍḍhas have held that what is cognised by the Abstract Cognition is only the '*svalakṣaṇa,*' the 'specific individuality' of the thing; (b) others have held the *summum genus, Saṭṭā,*' 'Being,' to be the object of Abstract Cognition; (c) others again hold that Abstract Cognition apprehends only the *verbal form* of things.

Such being the diversity of opinion, the truth, according to the Logician, is that as every Concrete Cognition is held to follow upon the corresponding Abstract Cognition, there must be some correspondence, some similarity, between what is apprehended by them. Proceeding from this standpoint we must reject the views indicated above.

(a) Firstly, the 'specific individuality' of things cannot be regarded as the object apprehended by Abstract Cognition; as when this is all that is apprehended by the Abstract Cognition, how can the notions of 'community' or class-character, come in, all of a sudden, into the corresponding concrete cognition? (b) Nor secondly could we accept 'Being' to be apprehended by Abstract Cognition; because as before, when the Abstract Cognition apprehends only 'Being' in general, how can the resulting concrete cognition become specified, all of a sudden? (c) Lastly, the verbal form of a thing cannot be held to be apprehended by Abstract Cognition; as it is absolutely impossible for any *verbal* form to be apprehended by a cognition brought about by the instrumentality of the Eye. The conclusion therefore is that what is apprehended by the Abstract Cognition is the same object that is apprehended by the corresponding Concrete Cognition; with only this difference that while the Concrete Cognition is accompanied by a verbal expression,—which appears in the representative Cognition 'I perceive the cow,' the Abstract Cognition is entirely devoid of any verbal expression. And just as the Concrete Cognition apprehends sometimes a substance, sometimes an action, and sometimes a quality,—exactly so does the Abstract Cognition also, with only the one difference just pointed out,—*viz.* the Abstract Cognition is free from all verbal expression, which however is inseparable from the Concrete Cognition.

Such is the view of the older Logicians. But from the *Taṭṭvachinṭāmaṇi* we learn that the chief difference between Abstract and Concrete Cognitions lies in the fact that while the latter apprehends its object along with its qualifying adjuncts, the former apprehends the object *per se,* by itself, independently of its qualifying adjuncts. The *Ṭaṭṭvachinṭāmaṇi* (p. 824) divides qualifying adjuncts into two classes which it calls (1) *vishēṣana* and (2) *upalakṣaṇa.* We lay stress upon this distinction as in course of our study of Indian Philosophy, this distinction will come up in many places; in some cases the whole argument turns upon the question as to whether a certain property is a *'vishēṣana'* or an *'upalakṣana.'*

That which is ever co-existent with the thing, and is inseparable from it is its *Vishēṣana*; while that which is not always co-existent with it, but is found to be so at some time or the other is its *Upalakṣaṇa* (Ṭaṭ. Chi. p., 834). So that *Vishēṣana* is the property or attribute of a thing, while *Upalakṣana* is only an adventitious adjunct. For instance, the tower of the Muir College is its *vishēṣaṇa*; but the presence of the All-India Hockey Games is an *upalakṣana.*

There are two other Cognitions which also the Logicians include under 'Perception.' One is the Intuitive Cognition that trained and advanced mystics have of things beyond the reach of the senses. These 'visions' cannot be dismissed as all false; for they are vouched for by persons of unimpeachable veracity; and yet they cannot be accounted for by any of the ordinary means of cognition. The Logician includes these under 'Perception' brought about by the contact of the internal organ of the Mind, through its faculty of 'intuition,' *Praṭibhā.* Says the *Nyāyamañjarī* (p. 105)—

'This Cognition is brought about by the instrumentality of the mind-organ, accomplished by the practice of meditation.'

The reach of the mind is not restricted, and when meditation is duly practised, its latent faculties becomes so far developed that its intuitive perceptive powers cease to be tramelled by the limitations of the physical body; so that its perceptive powers function unimpeded, and provide the perception of things, not perceptible by the physical organs under normal worldly conditions.

The second kind of cognition which the Logician includes under 'Perception' is *Praṭyabhijñā,* Recognition.

The exact character of Recognition is discussed in the *Nyāya-mañjarī* (p. 458 *et seq.)* and also in the *Ṭaṭṭvachinṭāmaṇi* (p. 839 *et seq.)*

Recognition appears in the form 'This is that same man whom I saw yesterday.' The question arises–Does this conception consist of two cognitions or of a single cognition? The Logician's answer is that there is a single cognition in this, though, what it apprehends is of a mixed character. This Recognition is brought about by the sense-organ–the Eye in the case cited–as aided by the impression left on the mind by the previous sight of the man; and what is apprehended is the object, the man, as qualified by the two points of time, past and the present. Nor is there anything incongruous in this. If the past time were apprehended as the *present,* or *vice versa,* the cognition would have been wrong; what happens however is that the *past* is apprehended as *past,* and the *present* as *present*–the cognitions meaning 'the man I see now, in the present, is the man whom I saw in the past;' and there is nothing wrong in this. As to how past things can enter into a present cognition, the *Nyāyamañjarī* cites a graphic example: When a man is eating mangoes, after he has eaten a few–25 *f.i.*–he has the idea 'I have eaten 25 mangoes,' or 'I am now eating the 25th;' both these conceptions must contain the idea of the twenty-four fruits already eaten, which are not present at the time of the cognition; as without the idea of these 24, the man could not have the notion of either 25 or of the 25th.

The *Ṭaṭṭvachinṭāmaṇi* (p. 839 &c.) deals with the nature of Recognition more minutely.

That Recognition is brought about by sense-contact is a fact that cannot be denied; and as such it has every claim to being called 'Perception.' As for the element of 'that'–'that I saw yesterday'–this is presented to the mind by remembrance; and this, being in contact with the mind as its qualifying factor, may be regarded as 'Perception.' The again, *because* the Recognition is related to the present time, that does not preclude all possibility of its being related to the past time; if it did, then there would be no possibility of our ever forming any conception of things related to several points in space.

Proceeding to analyse the notion of 'that' Gangēsha Upāḍhyāya offers three explanations: (1) when we perceive a thing, we cognise it always as related to the present time; similarly when we come to *remember* it we remember it as related to the past time; and it is in this latter form that we speak of the thing as 'that.' Even though the Cognition and the Remembrance both apprehend the same object, yet it is spoken of as 'that' only in Remembrance, and not in Cognition, in which latter it is always spoken of as 'this;' hence that which is referred to by the pronoun 'this' in connection with the Cognition is the same that is referred to by the pronoun 'that' in connection with the Remembrance; and so far as their *object* is concerned, there is no difference between Cognition and Remembrance.

(2) The second explanation of the notion of *'that'* is that it serves to signify the *past* character of that same qualification which is signified by 'this' in the conception 'this is the jar;' and even though this *qualification* has never been cognised as *past*, yet there is nothing incongruous in its being *remembered* as such; it is true that what has been cognised is the qualification as 'this,' pertaining to the present,--but we shall be justified in assuming that the impression left upon the mind by this cognition is in the form of 'that'; and after all Remembrance follows from the Impression.

(3) The third explanation is that in the Remembrance of '*that* jar,' what appears to consciousness in that connection, *with the present time,* is that which is qualified by the notion of

'that;' as what brings about the Remembrance is—not only the impression left by some past cognition, but,—the impression as aided by certain circumstances and accessories, appearing at the present time, and contributing to the idea of *present time* that appears in the Remembrance and consequent Recognition 'this is that same man.' Every reasonable man has to admit the fact that Remembrance and Recognition apprehend past time along with the *present;* if it were not so, no inference would be possible. When we infer the presence of fire from smoke, what happens is that when we see the smoke issuing, we are reminded of all the smoke that we have seen in the past, and found to be invariably concomitant with fire; and then taking this remembrance along with the smoke seen now,—we have the *recognition* of the smoke as that which has, in the past, been found to be concomitant with fire; and from this follows the inference that *there is fire in the place.*

Let us now consider in some detail the Vedanta view of Perception.

Perception, according to the *Vedānta,* is only *Chaitanya,* Consciousness, Intelligence. Though this Consciousness, constituting as it does the very nature of Brahman, is eternal, yet it is spoken of as 'produced' by the organs of sense, because of the fact that the *Vṛitti* of the Internal Organ (Mind), which serves to manifest that Consciousness, is produced by the contact of the organs of Sense; and hence it is the Consciousness qualified by the operation of the Mind that is said to be 'produced.' And the said operation comes to be called '*Jñāna*' 'Cognition', by reason of its serving the purpose of qualifying, or specifying or determining the Consciousness.

Question :- "The Internal Organ has no parts; how, then could it have any *vṛitti,* which is of the nature of *modification?* It is only a thing made up of several parts that could undergo any modification."

The reply to this is that the Internal Organ can not be without parts; as being a product, a caused Substance, it could not be without parts. And as such its modification would be quite compatible with its nature.

Nor is the Mind (Internal Organ) regarded by the *Vedantin* as a Sense-organ; and his reason for this is that if it were so, then we could not have any direct perception of it or of its modifications. Though it is not a Sense-organ, yet the cognitions produced by it,—such as those of Pleasure &c.—would be *direct* cognitions; because the directness (*Sākṣāṭṭva*) of a cognition does not consist in its being produced by the sense-organs; for if it did so, then Inferential Cognition also, being produced by the Mind, would have to be regarded as '*direct.*' According to the *Vedanta,* the 'directness' (*praṭyakṣaṭva* or *Sākṣāṭṭva)* of the Cognition consists in the unification of the *Cognitive- Consciousness (pramāṇachaiṭanya)* with the *Object-Consciousness* (the consciousness determined by the Object, *Viṣayāvachchhinnachaiṭanya).*

Chaiṭanya is of three kinds: (1) The *viṣaya-chaiṭanya* (Object-Consciousness), (2) the *pramāṇa-chaiṭanya* (Cognitive Consciousness), and (3) the *pramāṭṛichaiṭanya* (the Cognising Consciousness). To the first kind belongs the Consciousness determined by the object cognised, the jar *f.i.;* to the second belongs the Consciousness determined by the *Vṛiṭṭi* of the Internal Organ; and to the third the Consciousness determined by the Internal Organ itself.

The Internal Organ, which is of the nature of Light, passes out of the organs of sense, and having reached the object to be cognised, becomes modified into, and takes the form of, that object; and it is this modification which we call '*Vṛiṭṭi.*'

This *Vṛiṭṭi* does not appear in the case of Inferential and other kinds of Cognition. For instance, in the case of the inference of Fire from Smoke, the *Vṛiṭṭi* does not move up to the Fire, for the simple reason that it is not in contact with the Organ of Vision.

In the case of the perception of the jar, the Consciousness determined by the jar is found to be unified with that determined by the *Vṛiṭṭi* of the Internal Organ falling on that jar; in the same way as the *Ākāsha* enclosed within a vessel in the room, is unified with that enclosed within the room itself. And it is on account of this unification that the cognition of the jar, so far as the jar is concerned, is regarded as '*Praṭyakṣa,*' 'Direct'.

The following definition of the Internal Organ is in the main accepted by all Vedanta writers:

The Internal Organ is a Substance, and its material cause is Nescience; Īshvara, working in accordance with the previous actions of living creatures is its efficient cause. It is of middle magnitude; it consists of parts; and is neither atomic nor of infinite magnitude. Both the Internal Organ, and its qualities of Pleasure &c., are present to consciousness as being illumined by the Witness alone; *i.e.,* these are directly cognised by the Witness, without the aid of a sense-organ, or any process of Inference, though not without the aid of the *Vṛiṭṭi.*

As the Internal Organ functions like Light, its *Vṛiṭṭi* moves outwards in the form of an elongated ray of light; and hence like light-rays, this *Vṛiṭṭi* extends only up to a certain distance, where it stops short. This accounts for the non-perception of remote objects.

The Internal Organ is a material (corporeal) substance, and as such undergoes modifications of form. In all cognitions, this organ becomes so modified as to extend from inside the body to the object cognised. That part of the

Internal Organ which is within the body is what is recognised as "I" the *Cognising Agent;* that which exists as a ray of light extending from the body to the object is called the '*Vṛitti,*' the *action;* and that which extends over the object is called the 'Perceptible, *Object,*' inasmuch as it affords the objective of that cognition.

This tripartite Internal Organ being perfectly transparent, Consciousness becomes manifested or reflected in it.

Though this Consciousness is one only, yet on account of the Internal Organ reflecting it, it comes to be known as *three.* That Consciousness which is determined by the part of the Internal Organ known as 'Agent,' is the *Cogniser;* that determined by the Action-phase of the Organ is the *Instrument of Cognition;* and that determined by the objective phase of that Organ is the *Cognition.*

As all these three modifications are of the Internal Organ alone, it is only natural that we should have the notion that, 'this has been known by *me.*'

Though Consciousness is all-pervading (omnipresent), yet the cognition of one thing, or by one man, does not mean the cognition of all things, or by all men. Because we do not hold Consciousness to be the only cause of Cognitions; what we mean is that it is only Consciousness as qualified by the Internal Organ that can give rise to Cognitions; and the Internal Organ differs with each man; it is a limited entity, and as such cannot apply to all things in the world; it functions within well-defined limits.

The extent of these limits is regulated by the previous deeds of the man to whom the Organ belongs. When by Yogic practices one cleans his Karmic record, the limitations of his Internal Organ are cast off; and such a man is capable or perceiving all things at all times.

This does not reduce the Vedāntā theory to the Idealism of the *Bauddha.* Because what the latter holds is that Ideas or Cognitions have only a *momentary* existence; and the objects of cognition are not distinct from the cognitions themselves; while what the Veḍānṭin holds is that cognition is *one* and *eternal,* and objects are imposed *(aḍhyasṭa)* upon that Cognition, and are, each of them, capable of distinct, useful actions; and as such have an irrefutable existence. Cognition is one only; because whatever the objects of Cognitions, they are equally recognised as 'Cognition,' and the difference lies only in their objects.

Similarly too, the cognition of pleasure,—'I am happy'—is regarded as 'direct'; because in this case also, it is found that the Consciousness determined by the pleasure, as well as that determined by the *Vṛiṭṭi* of the Mind over that pleasure,—both of these are determined by the limitations subsisting in the same substratum. That is to say, the *Pleasure* and the *Vṛiṭṭi,* the two limitations of Consciousness, both subsist in one and the same substratum, and at one and the same time.

In the case of the remembrance of pleasure, the pleasure itself would be in the past, while the *Vṛiṭṭi* in the form of the remembrance would be in the present; and as such the two would not be coeval. Hence in order to exclude Remembrance, it becomes necessary to qualify the object of *Praṭyakṣa* as that which *exists in the present.*

Another qualification necessary would be *capability;* that is to say, *that which is capable of being perceived by the senses.* Otherwise the ideas of Virtue and Vice also would have to be regarded as *Praṭyakṣa;* and this by *Naiyāyikas* also; inasmuch as these are the qualities of the Self, just like Pleasure, Pain, &c., which they hold to be objects of *Praṭyakṣa.*

Thus then the character of *Praṭyakṣaṭva,* 'Direct perceptibility,' of an object consists in the fact of the

Cognition, determined by the *Vṛitti* of the form of that object, being unified with the Consciousness determined by that same object, which exists in the present, and is capable of being perceived by the particular sense-organ concerned.

Question: "How can the jar be regarded as unified with the Consciousness determined by the Internal Organ? We always have the idea in the form, *'I see this jar,'* where the Consciousness is distinctly differentiated from the Object."

Answer. What we mean by the 'unification' of the Jar with the *Cogniser* (Cognising Consciousness) is, not that the two are one and the same; but that the jar has no existence apart from the existence of the Cognising Consciousness. That is to say, the *existence* of the jar consists only in the existence of *objective consciousness* (*Viṣayachaiṭanya*) as super-imposed upon the Consciousness determined by that jar; the Vedāntin does not admit any imposed existence, apart from the existence of the substratum. This *objective consciousness* too is only the *cognising consciousness (pramāṭṛichaiṭanya)*, and the only existence that the jar can have consists in the *existence of the cognising agent*, which has that jar for its substratum. And hence it is that the cognition of the jar cannot but the *direct.*

In the case of Inferential and other kinds of Cognition on the other hand, inasmuch as the Mind does not move outwards to the object Cognised, the Consciousness determined by that object does not become unified with the Cognising Consciousness; and hence the existence of that object being distinct from that of the Cognising Agent, its Cognition is *indirect (parokṣa)*.

The *Vṛiṭṭi* itself is cognised directly, and by itself, not through any other *Vṛiṭṭi*; as in the latter case there would be no end of *Vṛiṭṭis*. And thus the properties of the Mind also become objects of direct Cognition, even though these are cognisable by the conscious agent himself, without the intervening agency of the organs; because every one of these properties has its corresponding *Vṛiṭṭi.*

Thus then the 'direct cognisability' or 'Perceptibility' of an object may be defined as consisting in the fact of its being capable (*yogya*), and devoid of any existence apart from the existence of the cognising Consciousness as affected (or qualified) by the *Vṛiṭṭi* having the form (or shape) of that object.

And the use of the six kinds of contact (enumerated by the Naiyāyikas) lies in the producing of the Vṛiṭṭi that serves to manifest the Consciousness (*Chaiṭanya).*

The *Vṛiṭṭi* is of four kinds: (1) *Samshaya* (Indetermination), (2) *Nishchaya* (Determination), (3) *Garba* (Self-consciousness), and (4) *Smaraṇa* (Remembrance).

And though the Internal Organ is one only, yet when it has the *Vṛiṭṭi* of Indetermination, then it is called 'Mind,' *(Manas)*; having the *Vṛiṭṭi* of Determination it is 'Will' *(Buddhi)*; with the *Vṛiṭṭi* of *Garba,* Self-consciousness, it is the 'I-notion' *(Ahaṅkara)*; and with the *Vṛiṭṭi* of *Remembrance,* it is *Chiṭṭa* (Attention).

According to the Veḍānṭin also, *Praṭyakṣa* is of two kinds: the *Savikalpaka* and the *Nirvikalpaka.* The former is the cognition pertaining to qualifications *e.g.,* the cognition 'I know the jar;' the *Nirvikalpaka* is that cognition which does not pertain to any relationships (of the object with any other factors), *e.g.,* the cognition produced by such sentences as 'That thou art' and the like. This latter cognition is not *verbal,* but *praṭyakṣa,* pure and simple, even though it is not produced by the Sense-organs. Because it has already been shown that the *praṭyakṣa* character of the cognition of an object consists, not only in its being produced by the sense-organs, but in the identification of the cognitive consciousness (*pramāṇa-chaiṭanya*) with the objective consciousness, following upon the object being capable of such cognition, and existing at the present time. And we find these conditions duly fulfilled by the cognition under consideration. As for instance, the 'Thou' is the same person to whom the sentence is addressed, and to whom the cognition born of it belongs; and as such there is an absolute identity, between the cogniser and the object cognised.

The Vedāntin makes another division of *Praṭyakṣa* into (1) *Jivaṣākṣi*—cognised by human consciousness, ạnd (2) *Īshavarsākṣi*—cognised by Divine Consciousness. By "Jīva" is meant the Consciousness determined or limited by the Internal Organ; and that which is cognised by this is the Consciousness presented to, or affected by, the Internal Organ.

This '*Jivasākṣi-Praṭyakṣa,*' on account of the diversity of the Internal Organs, is manifold, differing in each Self. The '*Īshvarasākṣi-Praṭyakṣa*' consists in the consciousness affected or conditioned by *Māyā* (Illusion); and this is one only, the conditioning *Māyā* being one. This *Māyā* being eternal, Divine Cognition also is eternal. The Consciousness qualified by *Māyā* is 'Īshvara,' God. When *Māyā* is the attribute, *Vishēṣaṇa,* of the Consciousness, it is called 'God;' and when we have *Māyā* as the conditioning or limiting adjunct of the Consciousness, then it is called '*Sakṣī*' (the Divine Cogniser). Though this God is one only, yet on account of the diversity of the attributes of *Saṭṭva, Rajas* and *Ṭamas,* in His qualifying *Māyā,* He comes to be known as '*Brahmā,*' '*Viṣṇu,*' '*Mahēshvara,*' and so forth. Just as in the case of our own Cognition various *Vṛiṭṭis* appear by the force of such causes as the contact of the object with the Sense-organs and the like, so, in the same manner, manifold *Vṛiṭṭis* appear in the *Māyā* conditioning this God, by the force of the *Karma* of the beings to be created by Him.

The name 'Praṭyakṣa,' as we have seen above, applies to the Object perceived, as also to the perception or cognition itself.

The general characteristic of *Praṭyakṣa-Cognition,* according to the Veḍānṭin consists in its *Chiṭtva* (Consciousness or Intelligence). This definition would apply to Inferential Cognition also, inasmuch as all cognitions are *Praṭyaksha, insofar as they themselves are concerned,* all of them being of the nature of *Consciousness.*

The object of such cognitions however can not be called *Praṭyakṣa,* as it does not fulfil the conditions described above.

This general definition would include misconceptions also; as these are as much *cognitions* as the right ones. Hence if we wish to exclude misconceptions from our definition, we must add the qualification that its object should be such as is not rejected or set aside by any subsequent cognitions, in the course of our ordinary worldly experiences.

Of *Brahma* also the Veḍānṭin provides his own characteristic explanation: When a man happens to have some sort of a derangement of the organ of perception, the Eye for instance, if he happens to see a thing, a piece of shell *f.i.,* there arises in his Internal Organ, through contact with the object before him, a *Vṛiṭṭi* in the form of 'This,' a something bright in appearance; in this *Vṛiṭṭi* becomes reflected the Consciousness qualified by the limitation 'This;' then, as explained before, the *Vṛiṭṭi* moves out of the body, and there comes an identification of the Consciousness qualified by 'this' with that qualified by the *Vṛiṭṭi,* and also the *cognising consciousness.* And then the *Aviḍyā*—in the form of the *shell* located in the *Objective Consciousness,* as identified with the *cognising consciousness,* aided by the impression of previously perceived *Silver,* and awakened by the perception of the quality of *brightness,* which is common to the *Shell* and the *Silver,*—becomes, by the influence of the derangement of the organ of perception, modified into the form of the *Object, Silver,* and also into the form of a 'dissembling cognition' of Silver. This silver, of the form of a modification of *Aviḍyā,* subsists in the *Consciousness qualified by 'this,'* which is the substratum of that *Aviḍyā.* And thus the actual *production* of silver, in the place of the shell, is as real as the production of anything in the world; because, in accordance with the *Vedānta* view, every effect subsists in the substratum of that *Aviḍyā* out of which it is produced.

The question that arises here is "How can there be any identity between the *silver,* which is located in the Consciousness, and 'this silver' which is before the eyes?"

The answer provided by the Veḍānṭin is as follows: In accordance with the *Nyāya* view, Pleasure and Pain, existing in the *Self,* are cognised as existing in the *Body,* simply because the Body qualifies their real substratum, the Self. And in the same manner, as pure Consciousness cannot be the substratum of the silver, and as it is only the Consciousness qualified by 'this' that can be its substratum, the *silver* becomes a qualification of 'This;' and there thus arises the notion of the silver being related to that which is before the Eyes. And this objective consciousness being identical with the consciousness *impinged* on the Internal Organ, though the Silver is only imposed upon the Objective Consciousness, yet it comes to be imposed upon the *Sākṣi* (the 'Witness,' the Cognising Self); and thus becomes known as something cognisable, like Pleasure &c., by the Self alone.

Nor would the fact of the silver being imposed upon the Cognising Self give rise to any such notion as 'I am silver,' or 'I *have* silver'—in the case in question. Because the object cognised is always in that shape which forms the object of the Impression or Idea aiding the *Aviḍyā* in bringing about that Cognition. Hence (1) ordinary objects, like the jar, are objects of the cognition in the form of 'This,' because of their being effects of *Aviḍyā* aided by impressions in the form of 'this;' (2) the Internal Organ &c., become objects of Cognition in the form of 'I,' because of their being the effects of *Aviḍyā* helped by impressions in the form of 'I;' and (3) the Body and the Sense-organs are the objects of cognition both in the form of 'This,' and in that of 'I,' because of these being the effects of *Aviḍyā* aided by impressions of cognitions in both these forms. It is for this reason that with regard to the Body we often speak as 'This' and also at times as 'I,' identifying ourselves with the Body.

In the case of ordinary misconceptions, *e.g.* that of Silver in a piece of shell, though the *apparent* or *dissembling* silver is the effect of *Aviḍyā* located in the Consciousness determined by the factor of 'this,' which is identical with the cognising Consciousness,—yet, the idea that 'this is silver' becomes the object of the cognition in the form of 'this,' because of its being produced by the Impression of 'this' left by the cognition of that form, in the case of real silver perceived elsewhere; and hence the cognition could not be in the form of 'I am silver.'

A *Bhrama,* 'Misconception,' is regarded as such because of its consisting in that Consciousness reflected in the two *Vṛiṭṭis* which identifies in itself the real and the unreal.

Though, according to the Veḍānṭin what is regarded as *real* silver is also an effect of *Aviḍyā*, and as such devoid of true reality, and in reality this is as unreal as the silver cognised in the piece of shell,—yet there is a very real difference between the two; inasmuch as the sole cause, and the only ground for unreality, of the ordinary cognition of silver, lies in *Aviḍyā* pure and simple; whereas the

Misconception of Silver in the piece of Shell is due to *Avidyā*, and also to some derangements in the perceiving organ. This difference has been thus stated: "Misconceptions are due to accidental causes, like the derangement of the organs &c., while ordinary cognitions are due to the natural and permanent nature of *Aviḍyā*."

It is thus that Dream-Cognition is regarded as 'False;' because of its being due to the *accidental* discrepancies induced by sleep. Dream-Cognition cannot be regarded as the effect of Memory pure and simple; as it does not appear in the form of a *remembrance*, as that 'I have seen such and such a thing at some previous time'—but it appears in the form of direct cognition—as that 'I see such and such a thing.'

It is Consciousness itself which forms the substratum of the objects created by fancy during dreams.

The Veḍānṭin also puts forward another Division of *Praṭyakṣa* into the following two kinds: (1) that produced by the Sense-organs and (2) that not produced by the Sense-organs. To the latter class belong the cognitions of Pleasure &c.,—as the character of 'Senseorgan' has been denied to the Mind, which is admitted by all as the means of cognising Pleasure &c.,—*V. Paribhāṣā*, p. 20.

There are five Sense-organs—of Smell, of Taste, of Vision, of Hearing, and of Touch. Every one of these produces Sense-Cognitions only when it is in contact with its object. Of these the Organs of Smell, Taste and Touch bring about their respective cognitions, while they themselves remain fixed in their own places in the body; those of Vision and Hearing however move out to their objects and then apprehend them. Hence it is not necessary to assume the fact of Sound being produced in waves that ultimately strike the tympanum and make the sound *heard*.

All Means of Knowledge have two kinds of validity (a) consisting in making known things having ordinary assumed existence, and (b) consisting in making knwon things having real existence.

The latter kind of validity belongs only to such as bring about the knowledge of Brahman. All others have the validity of the former kind alone.

(1) The *Bauddhas* hold that it is the sockets in the body that constitute the Sense-organs.

(2) According to the *Mīmamsāka* they consist in the faculty of potency attaching to these sockets.

(3) Other theorists hold that they are distinct from both of these, and are distinct substances by themselves.

The Veḍānṭin does not accept the 'socket-theory,' because he finds in certain animals,—in the Serpent *f.i.*,—that they can hear even though they are not possessed of the 'Ear-socket,'—and the trees, which are believed to be precipient living beings, are found to have no sockets for any organs.

For the same reasons, the Mīmāsāka-theory also has been discarded.

The third theory is that the Sense-organs are distinct substances, which, when related to the particular sockets in the body, come to be known as the 'Eye' and the rest.

But this, too, is not acceptable; as there are no grounds for believing in the existence of any such distinct substances.

With a view to these arguments some people have been led to deny the existence of Sense-organ altogether.

But on the authority of the Scriptures the Veḍānṭin believes the sense-organs to be something wholly different from the Sockets.

(1) The Sānkhyas hold that Sense-organs are the products of *Ahaṅkāra.*

(2) The Naiyāyikas hold them to be material products.

Though there are no sound reasons in support of this latter view, yet the Veḍānṭin also is led to accept it, on the strength of scriptural passages.

The *Yogas* hold that the Sense-organs are all-pervading in their character. But if they had this character, then we would have cognitions of all objects at one and the same time, as the Self is also omnipresent.

For this reason we regard the Sense-organs to have a limited existence only.

The Bauḍḍhas have held that the Sense-organs function towards bringing about cognitions of objects, without actually moving out to, and getting at, those objects.

But if such were the case then we could also touch and taste objects, without these objects coming into actual contact with our body,—which is not found to be the case. Nor could the theory be held to be true with regard to the organs of Hearing and Sight. Because we have no arguments to prove this. As a matter of fact, as regards the organ of sight, the nature of Light is such that no sooner is the Eye opened than the rays of light issuing therefrom at once move out and impinge upon the objects that fall within their range; and as for Sound, we do not hold that it is generated in the form of waves, which in their onward move, actually reach the Ear and are then perceived; because in that case we would cognise the Sound as '*in the Ear,*' and not as *in the place of its generator,* as we actually cognise it. Hence in the case of Sound-perception also, we hold that it is the Sense-organ itself that moves out to the object.

Thus then, we conclude that the Sense-organs are *material, limited,* and function by moving out to their objects.

What then is the Mind?

The Naiyāyika, as we have seen, holds that it is without parts, atomic in its dimensions, and eternal.

But the Veḍānṭin does not regard it as either impartite or eternal; and being partite, it cannot be atomic. Nor is it all-pervading, as that would lead to the possibility of all cognitions appearing at one and the same time. Hence he holds the Mind to have a medium demension—that it is neither atomic nor all-pervading.

According to the *Bauḍḍha* the Mind is nothing more than the idea that immediately precedes, and is the means of, Cognitions.

But this is not correct. Mere precedence of one cognition to another cannot make the one the cause or means of the other.

For these reasons we conclude that the Mind is a partite material and something wholly different from Cognitions produced by them.

*Some people have objected to the Veḍānṭic theory of *Vṛiṭṭi.* They argue as follows:

"Inasmuch as all things are capable of being illumined by the *prasāḍa* of the Witness, what is the use of the *Vṛiṭṭi?* Even though it may be necessary to postulate the *Vṛiṭṭi* for the sake of the treasuring of the impression *(Samskāra)* of such objects as the jar and the like,—yet there can be no necessity for admitting its *moving outwards.* For, just as in the case of an object not present to any Sense-organ, so also in the case of

*Vide *Siḍḍhānṭatēsha,* Trans. Venis; p. 744 *eṭ seq.*

an external object present to a sense-organ, the 'illumination' can be explained as due entirely to the Witness, which is in relation with a *Vṛiṭṭi* that has not moved outwards from the body of the observer. And in accordance with this view the difference between perceptional and non-perceptional Knowledge may be explained by the fact of the instrument of the former being the sense-organs, and in the latter something other than these."

There are three opinions in regards to this point.

(A) In a case of perceptional knowledge, the light that illumines the object is that Intelligence which underlies the object; for as being the reality that supports the object that Intelligence is the object; and the relation named 'Identity' '*tāḍāṭmya*' is directly possible. That is to say, in the case of an object that has been brought into immediate contact with the psychological apparatus by means of the outward movement of the *Vṛiṭṭi* of the Inner-organ, the relation may be regarded as that of Identity, the Identity of Essence; for the *Being* of the *object* is nothing but the *Being* of the *Knower,–viz.*, the Intelligential Principle; as it underlies the *Vṛiṭṭi* that, moving outwards, has fused with the object. This relation is said to be direct, because there are really not two correlates (in the relation), but only the one Intelligential Principle which appears as if it were two. Then as to the case of a non-presented object;–*i.e.*, in the case of an object not *seen* but *inferred,*–the Veḍānṭin finds himself compelled to fall back upon the ultimate fact that by *its own nature* the Witness can, and does, illumine into consciousness that object. This 'nature of a thing' is described as a relation, *Svarūpasambanḍha*, which is termed 'indirect,' as it is conceived not as in identity of Essence, but as a relation between two correlates, the Witness and the Object known. In accordance with this view the outward movement of the Inner Organ would be necessary for disclosing the Intelligence underlying the object,–*i.e.*, in removing Nescience that conceals this Intelligence.

(B) Other writers teach that, since our direct consciousness of the Inner Organ and its attributes, Pleasure &c., is due to all these being in direct relation with the Principle of Intelligence underlying them,—it must follow that the cause of our direct consciousness of external objects is only that Intelligence which is in direct relation with such objects, and that therefore the outward movement of the *Vṛiṭṭi* is necessary to disclose the Intelligence that underlies these external objects.

(C) Some other writers maintain the following: In the case of an object directly perceived through the senses, we are conscious of a certain *vividness, 'spaṣṭaṭā,'* as compared with an object known through other means of knowledge. Thus though a trustworthy person might describe the *sweetness* of the mango, the *vividness* of the direct sensation of taste will be absent. This *vividness* of the object directly perceived through the senses is due to the fact that the self-luminous, unchanging Principle of Intelligence, which is disclosed by the *Vṛiṭṭi* that has moved outwards, is identical in essence with the object perceived. That is to say, the necessary condition of vividness in the object is disclosure of the *Viṣayachaiṭanya,* and this *disclosure* consists in the removal of the concealing Nescience; and this can be accounted for only on the supposition that the *Vṛiṭṭi* moves outwards to the object. This vividness cannot be present in the case of objects perceived by other means of knowledge; because in the case of these latter, no *Vṛiṭṭi* moves outwards to the object, and hence the identity of the object and the Intelligential Principle is not *disclosed.* The consciousness of Pleasure and other attributes of the Inner Organ is *vivid,* as these are illumined by the Witness.

In accordance with all the above three views, the outward moving of the *Vṛiṭṭi* is ncecessary for the destruction of the Nescience concealing the object; and it has been urged that by the same arguments it might be proved that the *Vṛiṭṭi,* without moving outwards, would destroy the Nescience that pertains to and conceals the Intelligential Principle underlying the object of knowledge.

But if the outward movement of the *Vṛiṭṭi* be not admitted, no cause can be assigned for the fact that Knowledge and Ignorance are destructive of each other. Nor will the Principle itself suffice; for then it would follow logically that non-perceptional knowledge also could destroy the Nescience that conceals the peculiar character of the object, whereas, in fact, although one may have gained an indirect knowledge of the object, he would still desire to know its peculiar character.

'*Āparokṣya,*' 'Immediateness,' of a knowledge cannot be said to consist in the fact of that knowledge being effected through some organ of Sense. This definition will not apply to that immediate Knowledge of Pleasure &c., which we gain without the mediation of any Sense-organ, and which is direct consciousness in the form of the eternal Witness. On the other hand, it will extend too far,—in the case of an object which is present to a sense-organ and has its qualifications known by Inference,—to the knowledge of these qualifications also.

Question: Why does not the *Jīva* illumine objects by its *Siddhāntatesa*-Trans., p. 37, own essential nature of Intelligence, without the aid of any *Vṛiṭṭi*, just as Īshvara illumines objects without such aid?

In regard to this there are three views.

(I) The Absolute or Brahma-Intelligence being identical with all things, as being their material cause, illumines them as in relation to Itself; whereas the limited Jīva-Intelligence, or personal consciousness, cannot thus illumine; for since Jīva has Nescience as its limiting condition, it is not the material cause of all things; and therefore it is not in relation with all things, even though, as *Intelligence,* it is of infinite magnitude; and it is so determined by its own nature that it is not in relation with the external objects, but with the inner organ. Thus when a modification, or material part, termed '*Vṛiṭṭi,*' of the inner organ, proceeding outwards through the Eye, or some other sense-organ, reaches the external object, and changing its own form, just as the ray of the eye suddenly changes into a long ray of light, enters into that of the external object,—then the *Jīva* dominates the *Vṛiṭṭi* and perceives the external object.

(II) A second view is that Jīva is of limited extent, as having the material Inner Organ for its limiting condition; and being thus limited, it is not in relation with external objects, which therefore it does not illumine. But when, through the intervention of a *Vṛiṭṭi* of a certain Inner-organ, there is disclosed the non-difference of the Brahma-Intelligence,—which is limited by the external object in relation with that *Vṛiṭṭi,*—from that Jīva-Intelligence whose limiting condition that Inner Organ is,—then that *Jīva* illumines the Object.

(III) A third view is that Jīva, though of infinite extent, is concealed by Nescience, and, as thus not stirring forth itself, does not illumine external objects. But when through the influence of the *Vṛiṭṭi* on a certain external object, an influence is also produced on the *Jīva,* whereby the concealment of the *Jīva* is removed, then *Jīva* is disclosed in that external object, and illumines that and no other object:

And since it is shown that Jīva illumines only that object which is in relation with a *Vṛiṭṭi* of the Inner Organ, it has been shown further that Jīva possesses limited knowledge—the movement of the *Vṛiṭṭi* outwards towards the object is considered necessary either to influence Brahma, or to disclose the non-difference of the Intelligence underlying the object from that underlying the Jīva, or to overcome the concealment of Jīva by Nescience.

Question: (With regard to I above). What is the *influence* of Jīva brought on the perceived object through the *Vṛṭṭi* of the Inner Organ?

Answer: (a) Some writers hold that this Influence is nothing more than the relation of the Cogniser and the Cognised,—a distinct but *inexplicable* relation effected through the *Vṛṭṭi*.

(b) What takes place is an indirect relation between Jīva and the external object, effected through the contact of the *Vṛṭṭi* with the external object,—the *Vṛṭṭi* having become one with the Jīva-Intelligence which is its substrate, and which is in contact with the external object pervaded by the *Vṛṭṭi*. It is this indirect relation of identity of Jīva and external object that is meant by the said 'Influence' of Intelligence.

(c) Others hold that since we have an immediate knowledge of internal objects, such as Pleasure &c., which are in direct relation with Intelligence whose nature is Immediate Presentation, we ought to admit a direct relation with Intelligence in the case of perceptional knowledge of an external object. And since the *Vṛṭṭi* is found to be the determining cause in regard to the contact between itself and the external object, the relation of contact, between Jīva (which is the material cause of the *Vṛṭṭi*), and the external, object (as determined by that *Vṛṭṭi*), becomes also possible, this contact being brought about by the prior contact of the *Vṛṭṭi* with the external object.

(d) Others hold that the said *Influence* consists in the effecting of the identity of the external object with the Intelligence which, as limited by an inner organ, illumines all objects,—such identity being effected through an intervening process,—*viz.*, the disclosure of Jīva's oneness with the Brahma-Intelligence, which is identical with external objects. They argue, that, although Jīva, as of infinite extent, is in relation to all things and illumines them, yet in consequence of Jīva being common to all persons, it will follow that no explanation can be given of the fact of perceptional knowledge occurring to one individual, and not to another, at the same time; and therefore, to explain this fact, it must be held that Jīva illumines external objects only when it is limited by an inner organ (which is not one and the same in all persons). And in accord with this view, they urge, is the settled tenet of the Vedanta,—*viz.*, that in regard to direct knowledge of an external object, the determining cause is the relation of identity, erroneously surmised, between Cogniser and thing cognised.

Question: "What is meant by the 'disclosure of non-difference' (in view II)?"

(a) This disclosure consists in the fusion of Jīva-Intelligence underlying the Inner-organ with Brahma-Intelligence underlying the external object. This fusion is effected by the *Vṛiṭṭi* of the inner organ. Though it is Brahma alone which, limited by the external object, illumines it, yet Brahman becomes Jīva, or the personal Consciousness, when by means of the *Vṛiṭṭi*, it has become one with the Intelligence limited by the Inner Organ, and thus Jīva can be held to illumine the external object.

(b) The disclosure consists in the reflection of Brahma cast on the forepart of the *Vṛiṭṭi*, fusing into Jīva. The two cannot become one so long as the limiting condition is present in one. The process is explained thus: From the Inner Organ, situated in the heart, proceeds a *Vṛiṭṭi* outwards to the external object in a continuous line, after the manner of a long ray of light darting from a sparkling gem. Thc forepart of this *Vṛiṭṭi*,—*i.e.*, the part in contact with the external object—being transparent receives a reflection from Brahma (present everywhere). This reflection of Brahma on the *Vṛiṭṭi* illumines the external object and becomes one with Jīva (to whom the Inner-organ belongs).

This fusion becomes possible because the *Vṛiṭṭi* and the Inner Organ of wihch it is a part can come to be falsely regarded as non-different from each other; and thus the reflexions cast upon them,–*viz.*, Brahma and Jiva respectively–can also be 'disclosed as non-different.'

(c) The said 'disclosure' consists in the fusion of the Intelligence underlying the external object with Absolute Intelligence. The illuminator of the external object is none other than the Intelligence which is the sbustrate of that object. Hence there is a fusion of the Intelligence, which is the substrate of the object, with the Absolute Intelligence (Brahma), to which the character of a reflected thing, or a reflexion, is accidentally applied.

Then in regard to the third view (III), we have to consider the meaning of the 'destruction of the Concealing Nescience.'

(a) Some people hold that this destruction is not the destruction of Nescience concealing all Intelligence, but only so much of it as is confined to the space occupied by the external object;–such destruction being effected by a perception limited to such object; just as the wide-spread darkness is destroyed *in part* by the light of the firefly.

(b) Others hold that what is meant by 'destruction' is simply the ultimate fact in regard to the nature of Nescience which conceals Intelligence in general, *i.e.,* that Nescience by its very nature, does not conceal that Intelligence which is limited by the external object, and which is in contact with a *Vṛiṭṭi* that has assumed the form of that object (and which thus becomes perceived).

(c) Other writers again hold that the Nescience of whose destruction, by such perception, one is conscious is not the Primary Nescience, मूलाज्ञान, which is the material cause of the whole phenomenal world,—but it is that Nescience which is a special condition अवस्था of the Primary Nescience that conceals the Intelligence limited by the external object. These *special conditions* are numerically as many as there are Perceptions.

These special conditions of Nescience conceal Intelligence only under the restrictive conditions of time; that is to say, when a particular cognition has arisen, there is destroyed that particualr Nescience which, concealing the given object, is itself conditioned by the *particular time* of the said cognition; while the remaining Nesciences continue to exist and conceal the *object as conditioned by other times.*

Other writers hold that the first cognition destroys only that Nescience which conceals the Intelligence underlying the given object (स्वरूप); whereas the second and succeeding cognitions destroy the Nesciences which conceal the object determined continuously in space and time. And thus it happens that when a cognition, of Chaiṭra *f.i.,* has arisen for the first time, such cognition consists in the assurance that Chaiṭra exists,—and it destroys Nescience in regard to him; though there still continues the Nescience with regard to the time and place of his existence.

Nescience is of two kinds: (1) that belonging to the *Object* and concealing it, and (2) that belonging to the *Knowing Subject.* And the former cannot be destroyed by any Mediate or Indirect knowledge: because in this case, the *Vṛiṭṭi* of the Inner Organ has not moved outwards from the body of the Knower, to meet the object. Though in the case of all kinds of knowledge, the Nescience belonging to the knowing subject is destroyed.

Others hold that there is only one kind of Nescience, that belonging to the Knowing Subject. It is like a film over his eye and as such conceals the object also.

In dealing with the perception of an external world, the *Siddhantatesha Trans.* Venis, p. 75, *Note.* Veḍānṭin falls back upon metaphysics, aided by the Metaphor of Illumination. Every form of existence (*Saṭṭā)* has its source in, or more strictly, *is,* the one principle of Self-luminous Intelligence. Existence cannot be predicated away from the Intelligential Principle. In all Knowledge, the ultimate predicate is this Self-luminous Principle. Hence all personal consciousness, involving as it does the duality of Subject and Object, must be regarded as a *false presentation* of this one Principle. *False,* for though it *appears,* no explanation can be given of its appearance; it remains inexplicable (अनिर्वचनीय), the work of *Māyā.* To the Veḍānṭin, therefore, the Psychology of Perception is an insoluble problem. And all that he attempts is to state the invariable circumstance or condition under which Sense-perception *appears* to occur.

The three commonly recognised elements of such experience he expresses in terms of his one real principle as (a) the Intelligence underlying the external object–विषयावच्छिन्न चैतन्यम्, (b) the Cogniser, the Intelligence underlying the Inner organ–अन्तःकरणावच्छिन्नम्प्रमातृचैतन्यम्; and (c) the Intelligence underlying the Instrument, or the *Vriṭṭi* of the Inner Organ–वृत्त्यवच्छिन्नम्प्रमाणातचैन्यम्. He draws attention to the ambiguity in the term *Perception,* as used both for the Cognitional Result following from a certain process, and the object cognised–as मम घटः प्रत्यक्षः and मदीयङ्घटज्ञानम्प्रत्यक्षम्. The invariable condition of the Cognition itself is that of *non-difference* between the Intelligence underlying the *Vriṭṭi* and the Intelligence underlying the external object. This *non-difference* or *fusion* of the two Intelligences is effected by the Vriṭṭi moving outwards and occupying the space as the Object. How this is possible in the case of a *material* body like the *Vriṭṭi* is not explained; but we may suppose that the *Vriṭṭi* is of so rare a nature that it can permeate the external object, just as fire penetrates the material body to which it imparts heat; [or, it may be of the nature of light-rays which falling on an object assume its *shape.*].

Then in regard to the external object, the Veḍānṭin holds that the invariable condition is that of its *non-difference* from the Cogniser—*i.e.*, from the Intelligence underlying the Inner Organ. To explain this non-difference or fusion again he has recourse to his one Real Principle. Thus, the Existence of the Object is the existence of the Intelligence underlying it; and this Intelligence has fused with the Intelligence underlying the *Vṛitti*; and therefore also with the Intelligence underlying the Inner-organ, of which the *Vṛiṭṭi* is a part; or, in other words, the Intelligence underlying the Inner Organ has become the substrate of the external object, so that the existence of this object has become the existence of the Cogniser?

This *non-difference* does not mean that the ***knower*** and the ***known*** are numerically identical (ऐक्यम्) for these always appear in consciousness as numerically distinct; but it means that the thing, ***as a thing known,*** has no existence apart from the Existence of the *Knower.*